The Celebrated Hans Holbein's Alphabet of Death

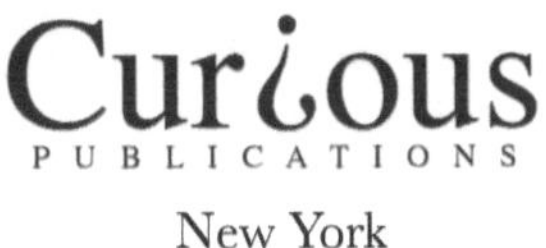

Curious

PUBLICATIONS

New York

Published by Curious Publications
101 W. 23rd St. #318
New York, NY 10011
curiouspublications.com

Copyright © 2021

ISBN-13: 978-1-7353201-2-0

Printed and bound in the United States of America.

A NOTE ON THE TEXT

This book is a reproduction of an 1856 edition put together by nineteenth-century French librarian and art historian, Anatole de Courde de Montaiglon.

Hans Holbein (1497-1543) created the Alphabet of Death at a time when the Latin alphabet did not distinguish between I and J or U and V—the separation into vowels and consonants came after the Renaissance. Therefore, you'll notice Holbein's alphabet has only twenty-four letters.

Further details are offered by De Montaiglon in his introduction to the book. Following the original edition, each letter of the Alphabet of Death is enlarged to allow a closer look at Hans Holbein's meticulously detailed work.

THE CELEBRATED

HANS HOLBEIN'S

ALPHABET OF DEATH

ILLUSTRATED WITH OLD BORDERS ENGRAVED ON WOOD
WITH LATIN SENTENCES AND ENGLISH QUATRAINS

selected by

ANATOLE DE MONTAIGLON

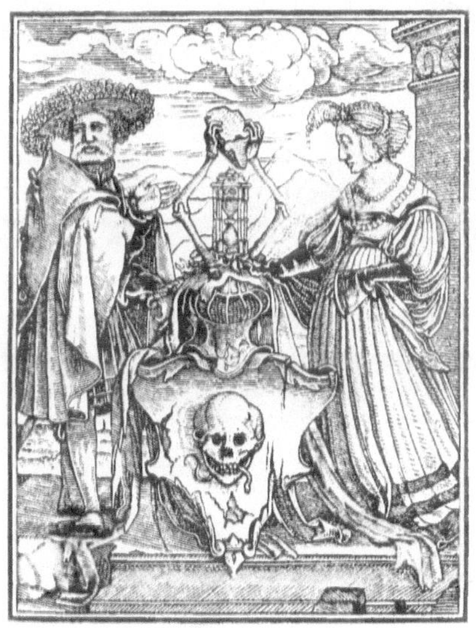

PARIS

PRINTED FOR EDWIN TROSS

28, Rue des Bons - Enfants

MDCCCLVI

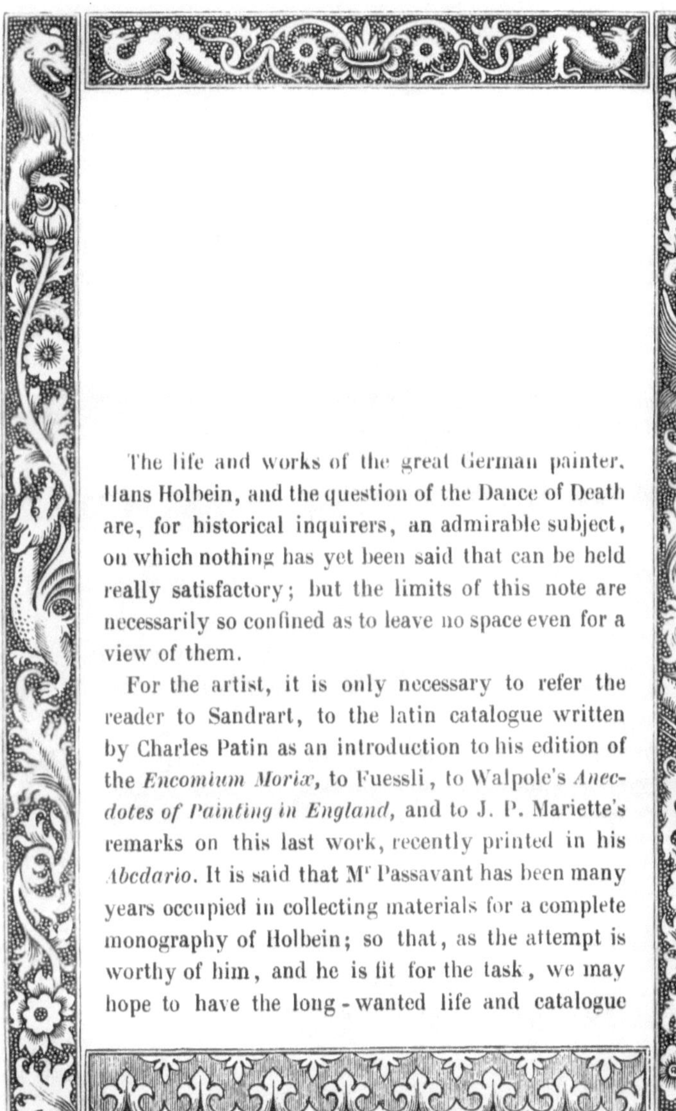

The life and works of the great German painter,
Hans Holbein, and the question of the Dance of Death
are, for historical inquirers, an admirable subject,
on which nothing has yet been said that can be held
really satisfactory; but the limits of this note are
necessarily so confined as to leave no space even for a
view of them.

For the artist, it is only necessary to refer the
reader to Sandrart, to the latin catalogue written
by Charles Patin as an introduction to his edition of
the *Encomium Moriæ*, to Fuessli, to Walpole's *Anec-
dotes of Painting in England*, and to J. P. Mariette's
remarks on this last work, recently printed in his
Abcdario. It is said that Mⁿ Passavant has been many
years occupied in collecting materials for a complete
monography of Holbein; so that, as the attempt is
worthy of him, and he is fit for the task, we may
hope to have the long - wanted life and catalogue

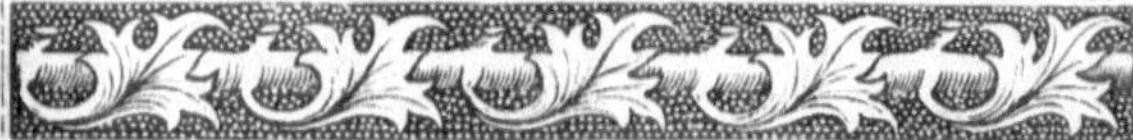

executed in a superior manner. On the Dance of
Death, several interesting books have been published,
among which it is almost unnecessary to name those
of Gabriel Peignot, Francis Douce, and Hyacinthe
Langlois. Here we have only to speak of the Alphabet
itself.

Engraved by Hans Lutzelburger, as now thought
by the most competent critics, it was first used at
Basle about the year 1530 by the famous printers Be-
belius and Cratander, and we refer to Douce's remarks (p. 214-18) on the question for the titles of the
books in which it was employed, and for the nume-
rous copies and imitations made of it. We will only
repeat with him that these initial letters, « in elegance of design and delicacy of engraving, have
scarcely ever been equalled, and certainly never sur-
passed. They may in every point of view be regarded
as the chef-d'œuvre of ancient block engraving. »

Seven years ago, in 1849, the whole series was
anew elegantly copied on wood by Professor H. Lö-
del of Göttingen, and published in a little 8vo vo-
lume, with George Osterwald's lithographed borders,
by I. M. Heberle at Cologne, Bonn and Brussels.
Our new edition gives the same letters, real gems
of engraving on wood, but, as a worthy illustration,
accompanies them with the two Dances of Death, the
one more Gothic in form, the other more coarsely
engraved, but yet perhaps more artistical, which are

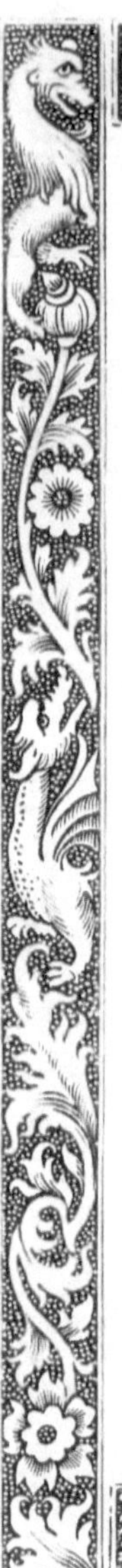

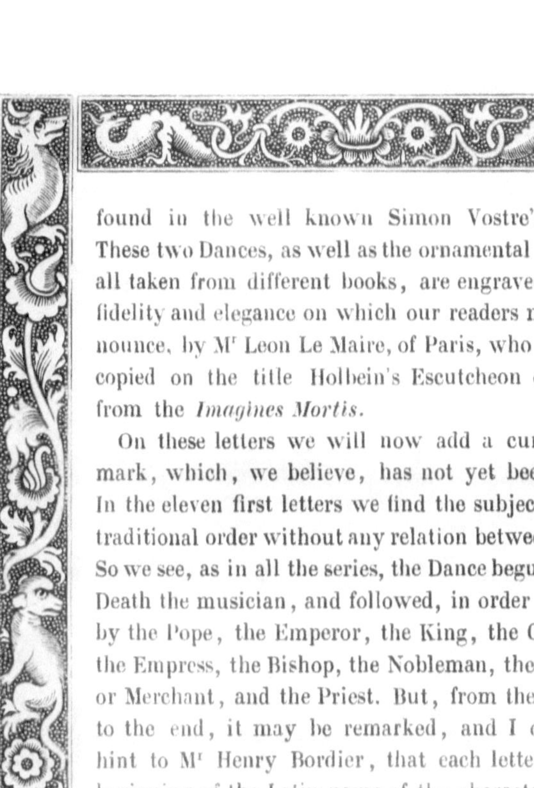

found in the well known Simon Vostre's *Horæ*. These two Dances, as well as the ornamental borders, all taken from different books, are engraved with a fidelity and elegance on which our readers may pronounce, by Mr Leon Le Maire, of Paris, who has also copied on the title Holbein's Escutcheon of Death from the *Imagines Mortis*.

On these letters we will now add a curious remark, which, we believe, has not yet been made. In the eleven first letters we find the subjects in the traditional order without any relation between them. So we see, as in all the series, the Dance begun by the Death the musician, and followed, in order of rank, by the Pope, the Emperor, the King, the Cardinal, the Empress, the Bishop, the Nobleman, the Burgess or Merchant, and the Priest. But, from the letter M to the end, it may be remarked, and I owe this hint to Mr Henry Bordier, that each letter is the beginning of the Latin name of the character represented.

So, at M we see the *Medicus;* at N the banker, *Numerarius;* at O a fat monk, *Obesus monachus;* at P a fighting soldier, *Præliator*. The Q is less clear; the obedient nun who quietly follows Death, might however be called in Latin : *Quieta, quassata,* or *queribunda monacha*. But the R is quite certain, for we find in it : *Ridens* or *ridiculus fatuus*. In the S we have the luxurious woman, *Scortum*. The T is

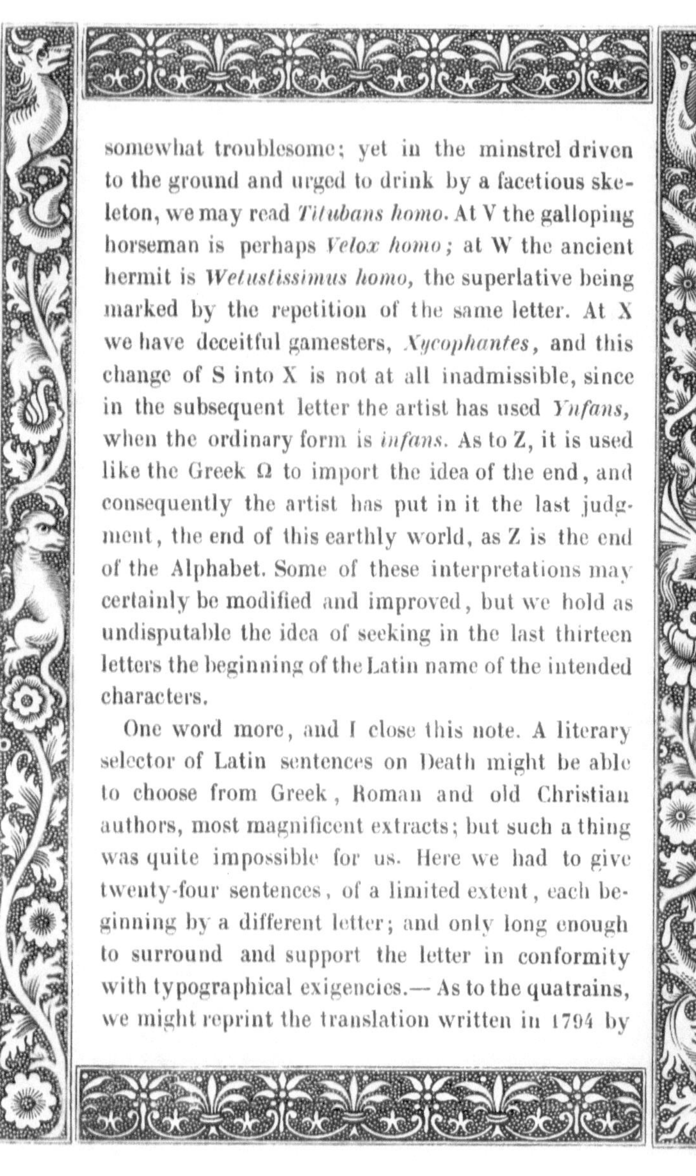

somewhat troublesome; yet in the minstrel driven to the ground and urged to drink by a facetious skeleton, we may read *Titubans homo*. At **V** the galloping horseman is perhaps *Velox homo*; at **W** the ancient hermit is *Wetustissimus homo,* the superlative being marked by the repetition of the same letter. At **X** we have deceitful gamesters, *Xycophantes,* and this change of **S** into **X** is not at all inadmissible, since in the subsequent letter the artist has used *Ynfans,* when the ordinary form is *infans*. As to **Z**, it is used like the Greek Ω to import the idea of the end, and consequently the artist has put in it the last judgment, the end of this earthly world, as **Z** is the end of the Alphabet. Some of these interpretations may certainly be modified and improved, but we hold as undisputable the idea of seeking in the last thirteen letters the beginning of the Latin name of the intended characters.

One word more, and I close this note. A literary selector of Latin sentences on Death might be able to choose from Greek, Roman and old Christian authors, most magnificent extracts; but such a thing was quite impossible for us. Here we had to give twenty-four sentences, of a limited extent, each beginning by a different letter; and only long enough to surround and support the letter in conformity with typographical exigencies.— As to the quatrains, we might reprint the translation written in 1794 by

Hawkins for his edition of a copy of Holbein's *Imagines Mortis;* but we have chosen to have them
made for the most part with the stanzas of the old
translation of the Macabre's Dance by John Lydgate,
and some new-written in the same style, so that
each may be indicative of the subject in the letter.
That is all that can be said on them.

A. DE M.

Paris, 12th July, 1856.

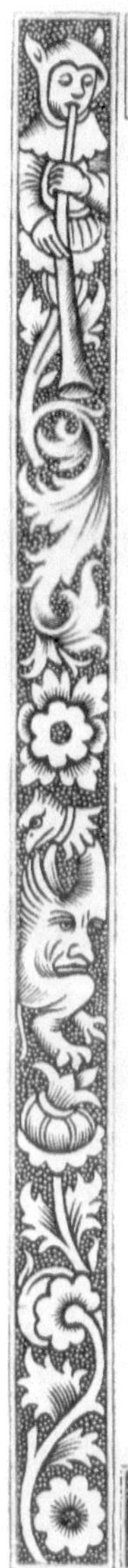

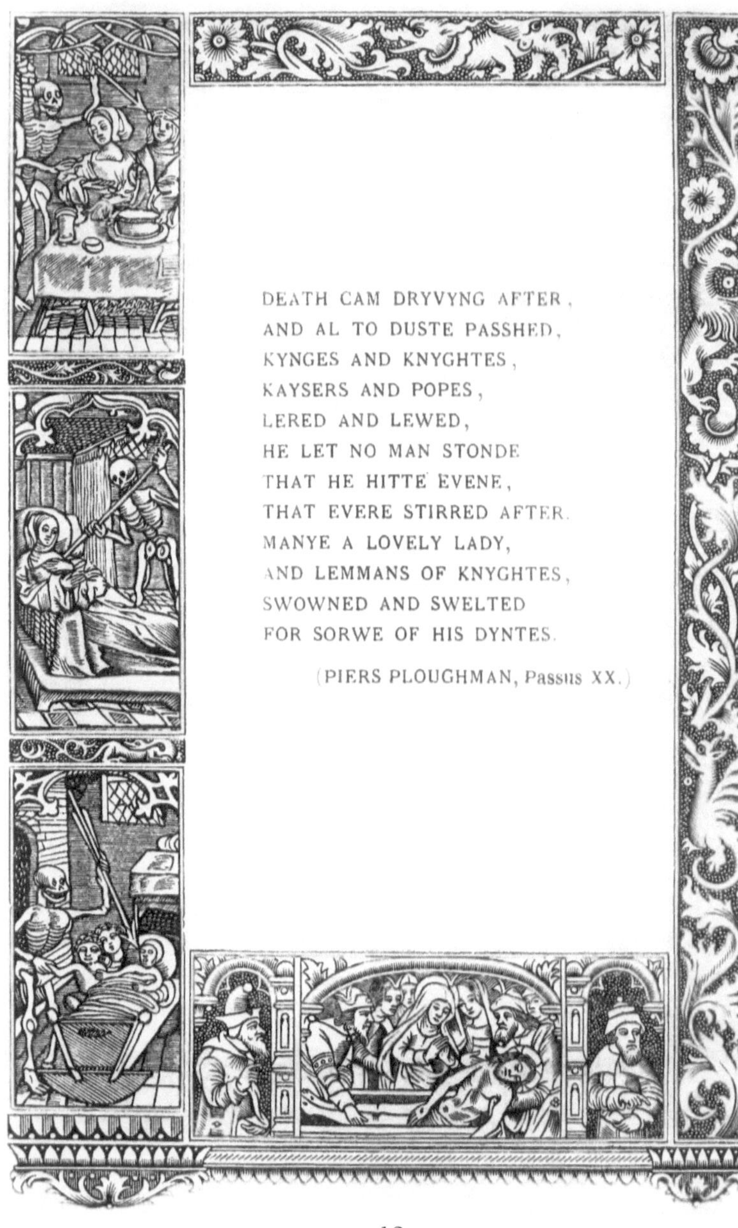

DEATH CAM DRYVYNG AFTER,
AND AL TO DUSTE PASSHED,
KYNGES AND KNYGHTES,
KAYSERS AND POPES,
LERED AND LEWED,
HE LET NO MAN STONDE
THAT HE HITTE EVENE,
THAT EVERE STIRRED AFTER.
MANYE A LOVELY LADY,
AND LEMMANS OF KNYGHTES,
SWOWNED AND SWELTED
FOR SORWE OF HIS DYNTES.

(PIERS PLOUGHMAN, Passus XX.)

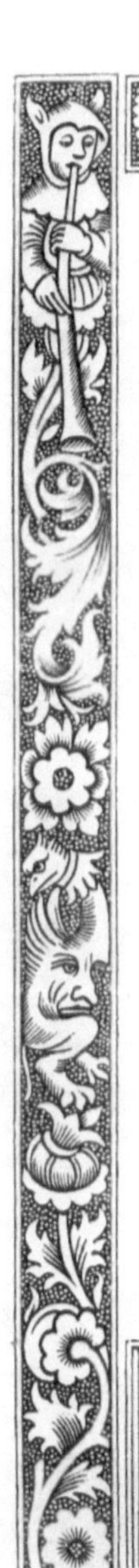

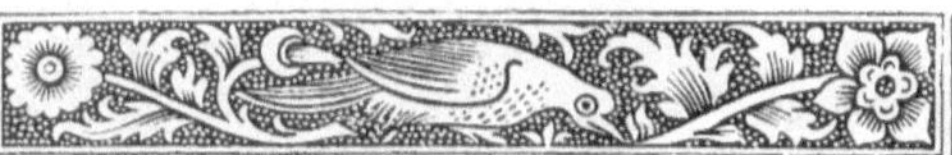

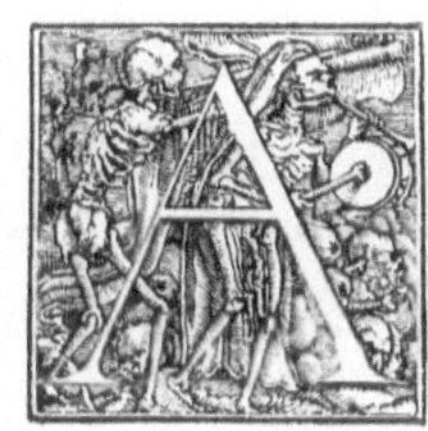Pud mortem non
est acceptio per-
sonarum. Nec mi-
seretur pupillo,
nec defert senio-
ri, nec timet potentem, nec vere-
tur nobilem, nec horret pauperem
aut ignobilem, nec dimittit divi-
tem aut potentem, nec contemnit
infirmem aut debilem, nec evitat
fortem, nec parcit sapienti, nec
insipienti.

S. ANTONINUS.

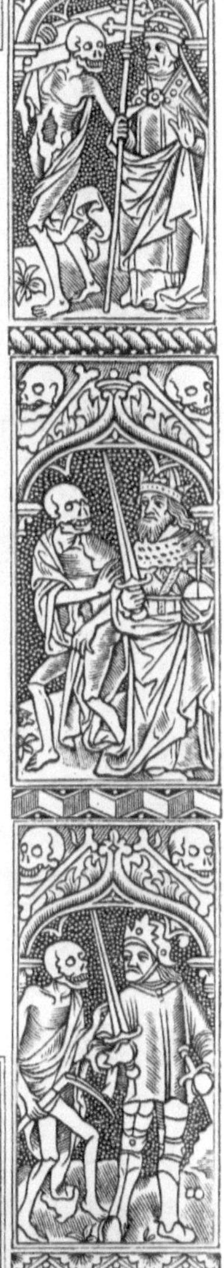

A 1

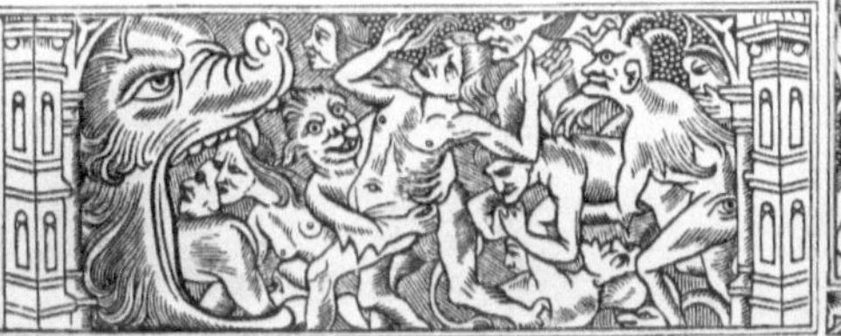

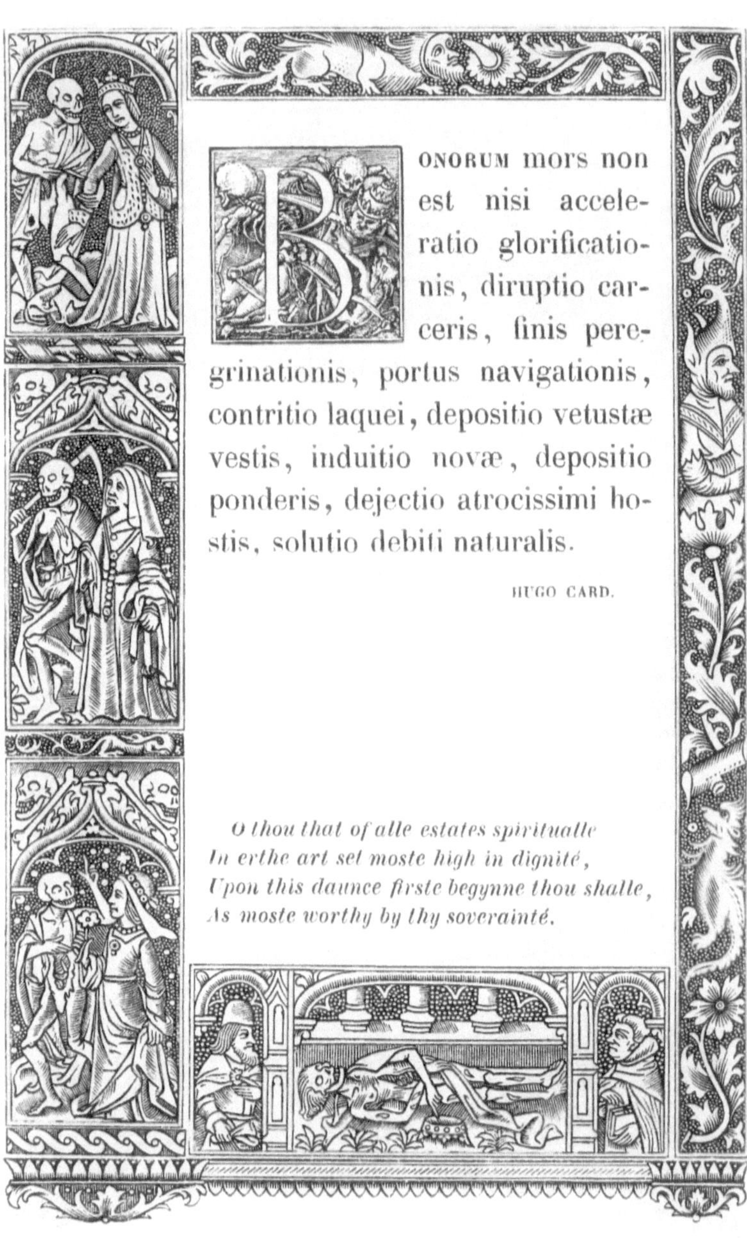

ONORUM mors non est nisi accele- ratio glorificatio- nis, diruptio car- ceris, finis pere- grinationis, portus navigationis, contritio laquei, depositio vetustæ vestis, induitio novæ, depositio ponderis, dejectio atrocissimi ho- stis, solutio debiti naturalis.

HUGO CARD.

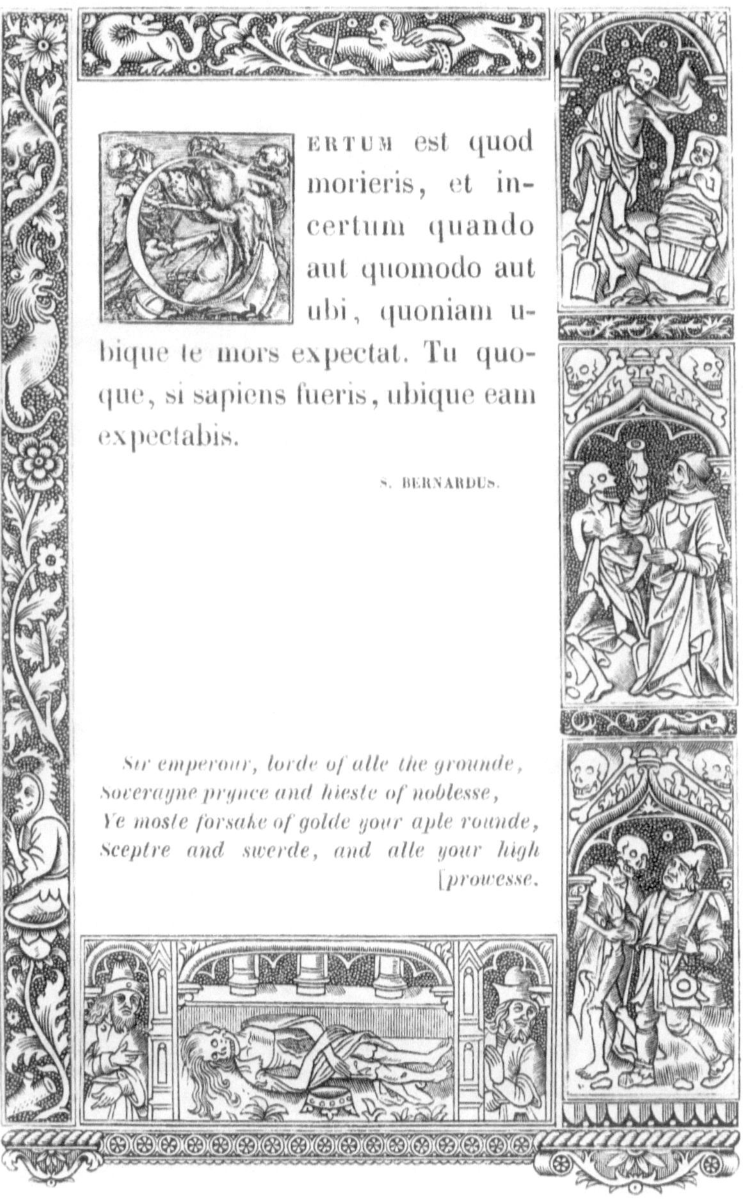

CERTUM est quod morieris, et incertum quando aut quomodo aut ubi, quoniam ubique te mors expectat. Tu quoque, si sapiens fueris, ubique eam expectabis.

S. BERNARDUS.

Sir emperour, lorde of alle the grounde,
Soverayne prynce and hieste of noblesse,
Ye moste forsake of golde your aple rounde,
Sceptre and swerde, and alle your high
[prowesse.

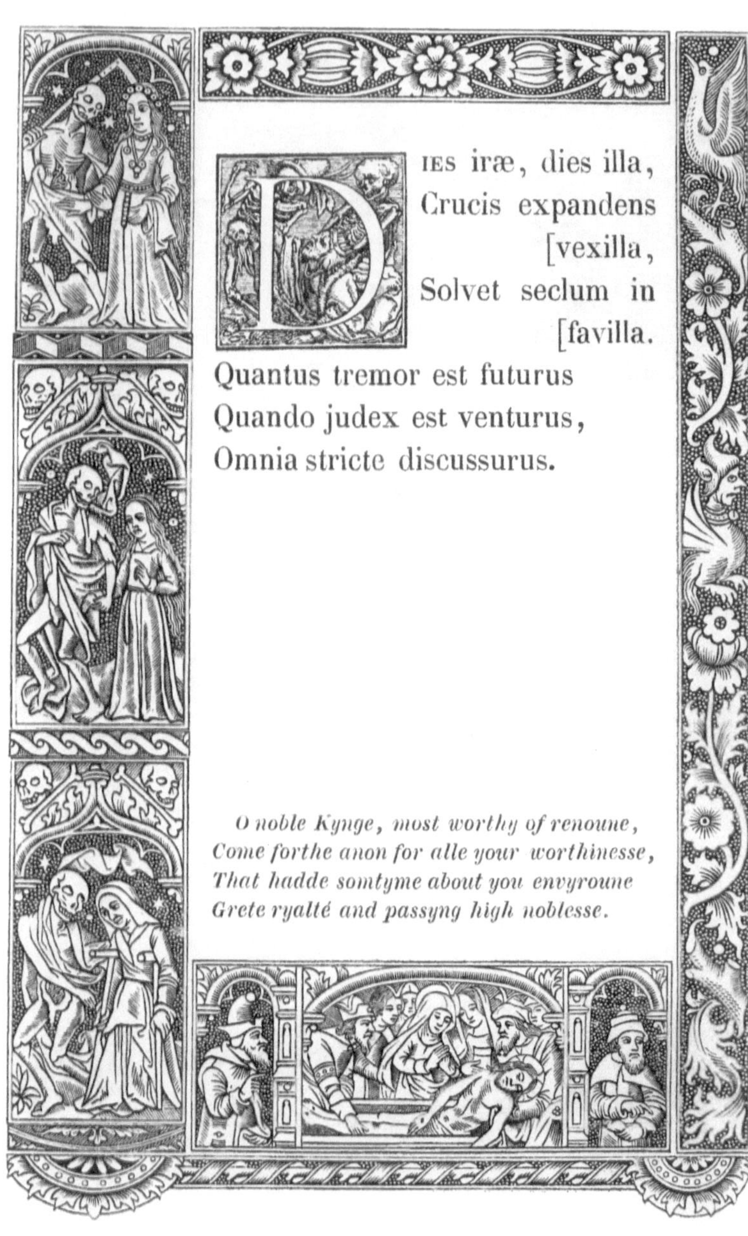

DIES iræ, dies illa,
Crucis expandens
 [vexilla,
Solvet seclum in
 [favilla.
Quantus tremor est futurus
Quando judex est venturus,
Omnia stricte discussurus.

O noble Kynge, most worthy of renoune,
Come forthe anon for alle your worthinesse,
That hadde somtyme about you envyroune
Grete ryalté and passyng high noblesse.

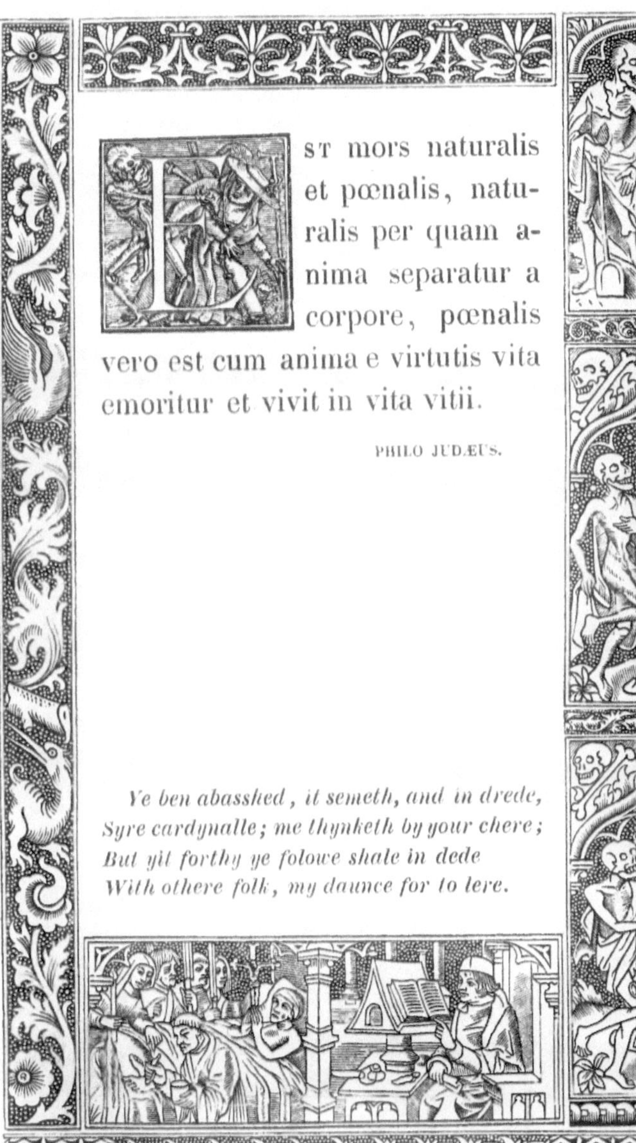

Est mors naturalis et pœnalis, naturalis per quam anima separatur a corpore, pœnalis vero est cum anima e virtutis vita emoritur et vivit in vita vitii.

PHILO JUDÆUS.

Ye ben abasshed, it semeth, and in drede,
Syre cardynalle; me thynketh by your chere;
But yit forthy ye folowe shale in dede
With other folk, my daunce for to lere.

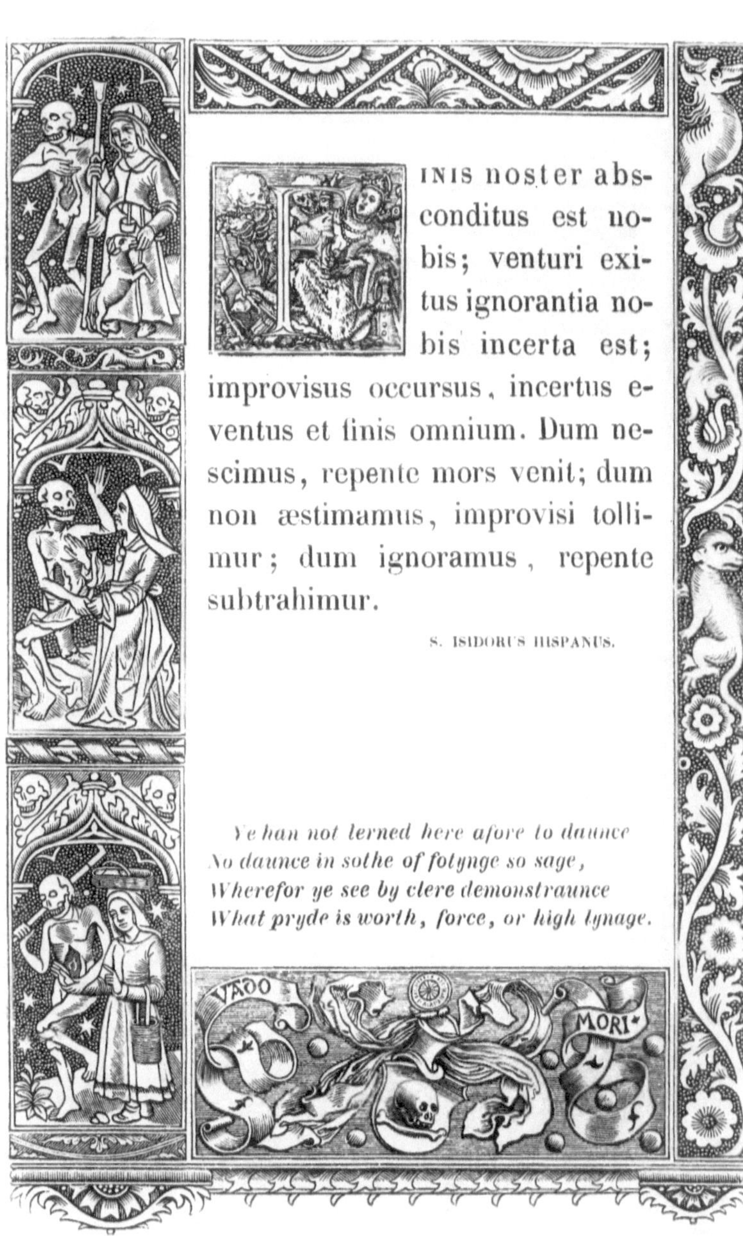

INIS noster absconditus est nobis; venturi exitus ignorantia nobis incerta est; improvisus occursus, incertus eventus et finis omnium. Dum nescimus, repente mors venit; dum non æstimamus, improvisi tollimur; dum ignoramus, repente subtrahimur.

S. ISIDORUS HISPANUS.

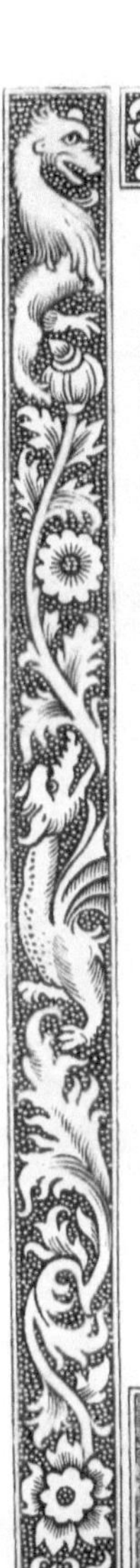

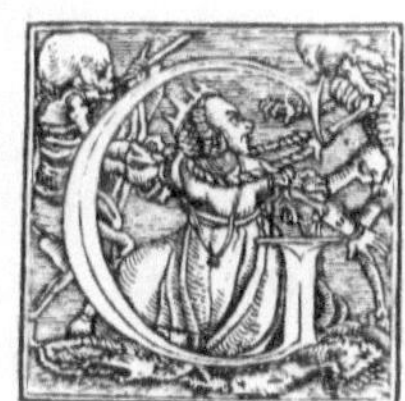 ERMANA corruptio-
nis mors est, de-
sperationis domi-
na, incredulitatis
mater, inferni pa-
rens, diaboli conjunx, omnium
malorum regina.

S. PETRUS CHRYSOLOGUS.

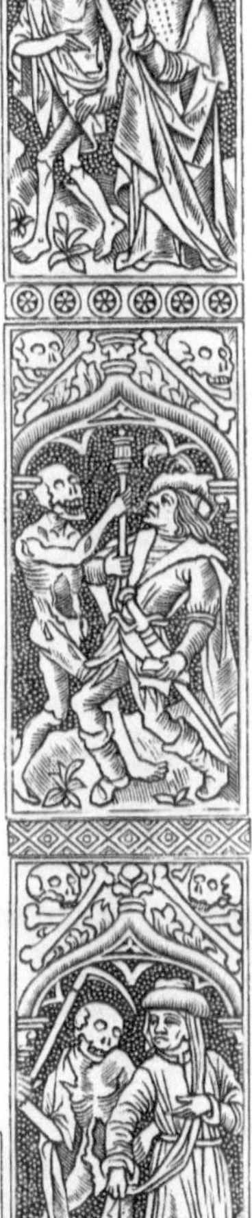

Madame, in sothe, ther is non other bote;
Dethe hath in erthe no lady ne maistresse,
But on this daunce ye moste nedis fote,
Al, be ye quene, countesse, or duchesse.

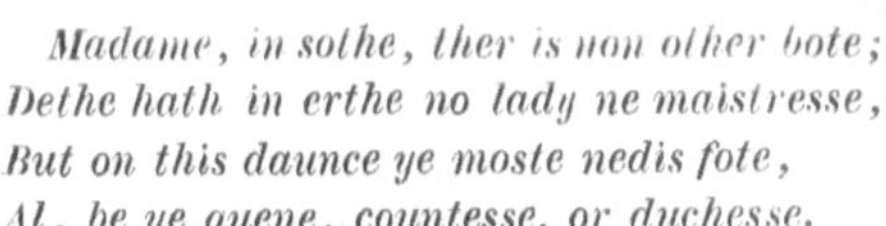

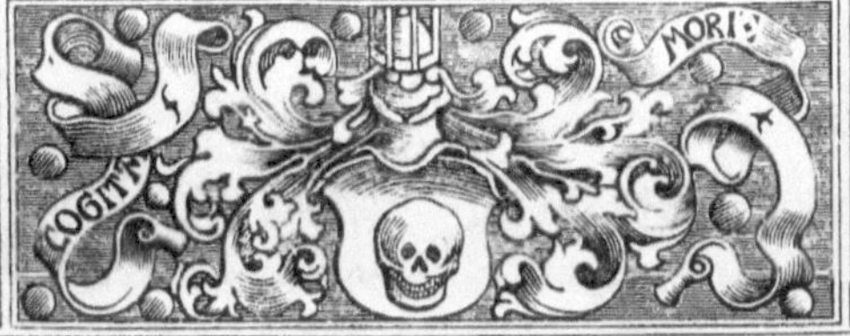

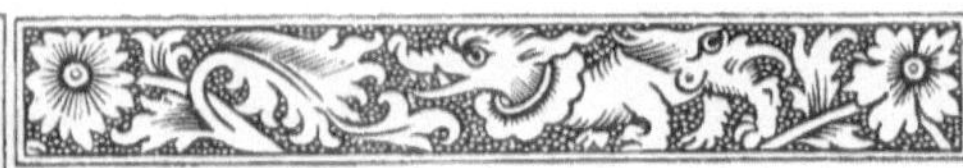

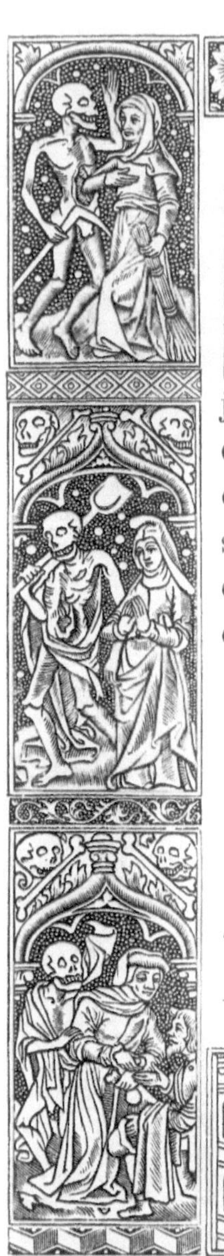

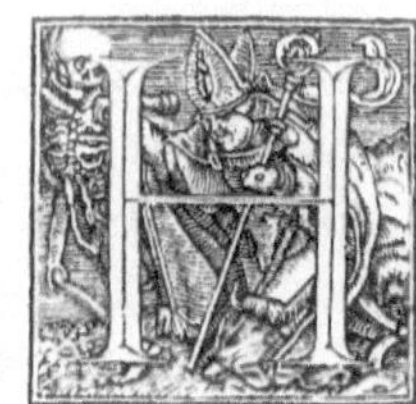 Æc paria sunt. Non eris, nec fuisti, utrumque tempus alienum est. In hoc punctum conjectus es : quod ut extendas, quousque extendes? Quid fles? Quid optas? Perdis operam. Rata et fixa sunt, atque magna et æterna necessitate ducuntur. Eo ibis quo omnia eunt.

SENECA.

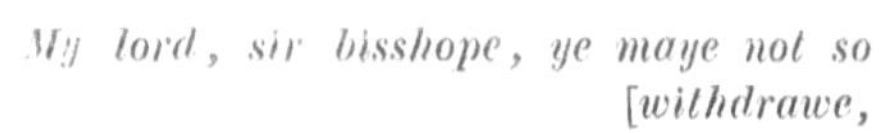

My lord, sir bisshope, ye maye not so
[withdrawe,
Se frowardly, as it were by disdeyne,
Ye moste approche unto my mortale lawe
It to contraire it were but in veyne.

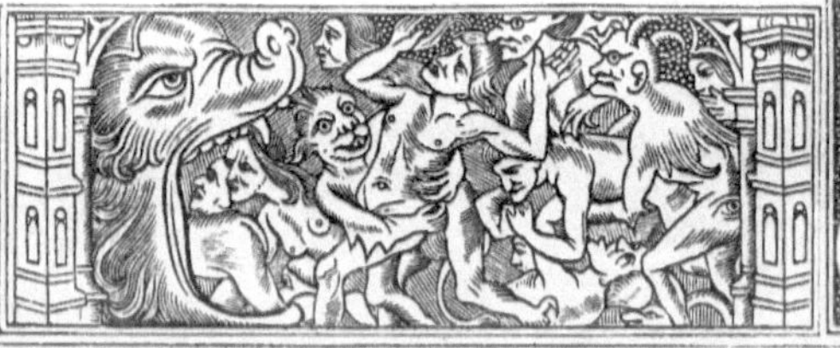

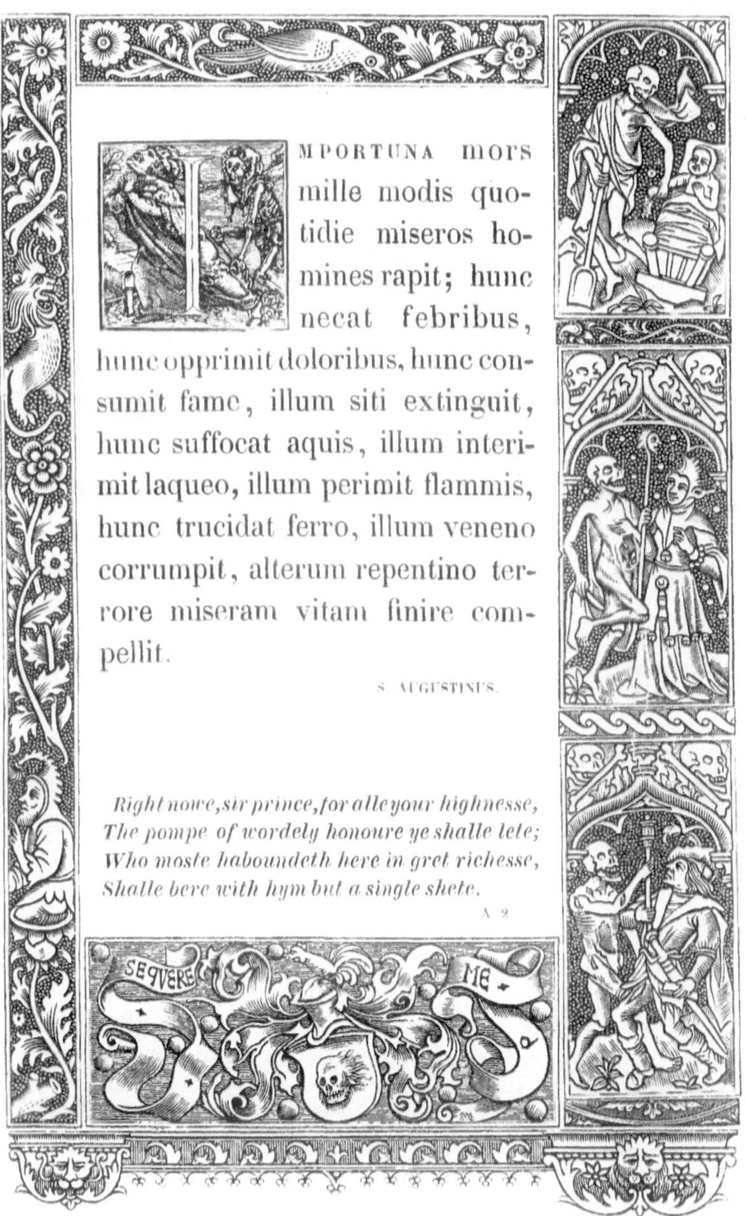

IMPORTUNA mors mille modis quotidie miseros homines rapit; hunc necat febribus, hunc opprimit doloribus, hunc consumit fame, illum siti extinguit, hunc suffocat aquis, illum interimit laqueo, illum perimit flammis, hunc trucidat ferro, illum veneno corrumpit, alterum repentino terrore miseram vitam finire compellit.

S. AUGUSTINUS.

Right nowe, sir prince, for alle your highnesse,
The pompe of wordely honoure ye shalle lete;
Who moste haboundeth here in gret richesse,
Shalle bere with hym but a single shete.

A 2

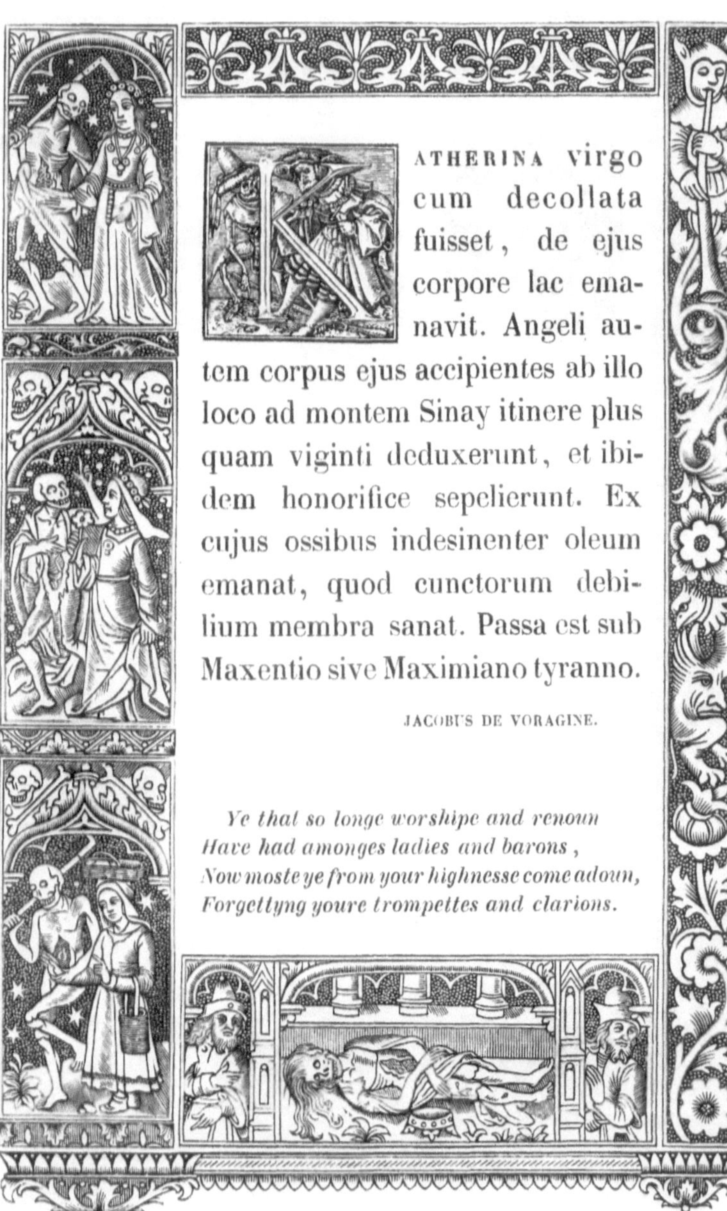

ATHERINA virgo cum decollata fuisset, de ejus corpore lac emanavit. Angeli autem corpus ejus accipientes ab illo loco ad montem Sinay itinere plus quam viginti deduxerunt, et ibidem honorifice sepelierunt. Ex cujus ossibus indesinenter oleum emanat, quod cunctorum debilium membra sanat. Passa est sub Maxentio sive Maximiano tyranno.

JACOBUS DE VORAGINE.

Ye that so longe worshipe and renoun
Have had amonges ladies and barons,
Now moste ye from your highnesse come adoun,
Forgettyng youre trompettes and clarions.

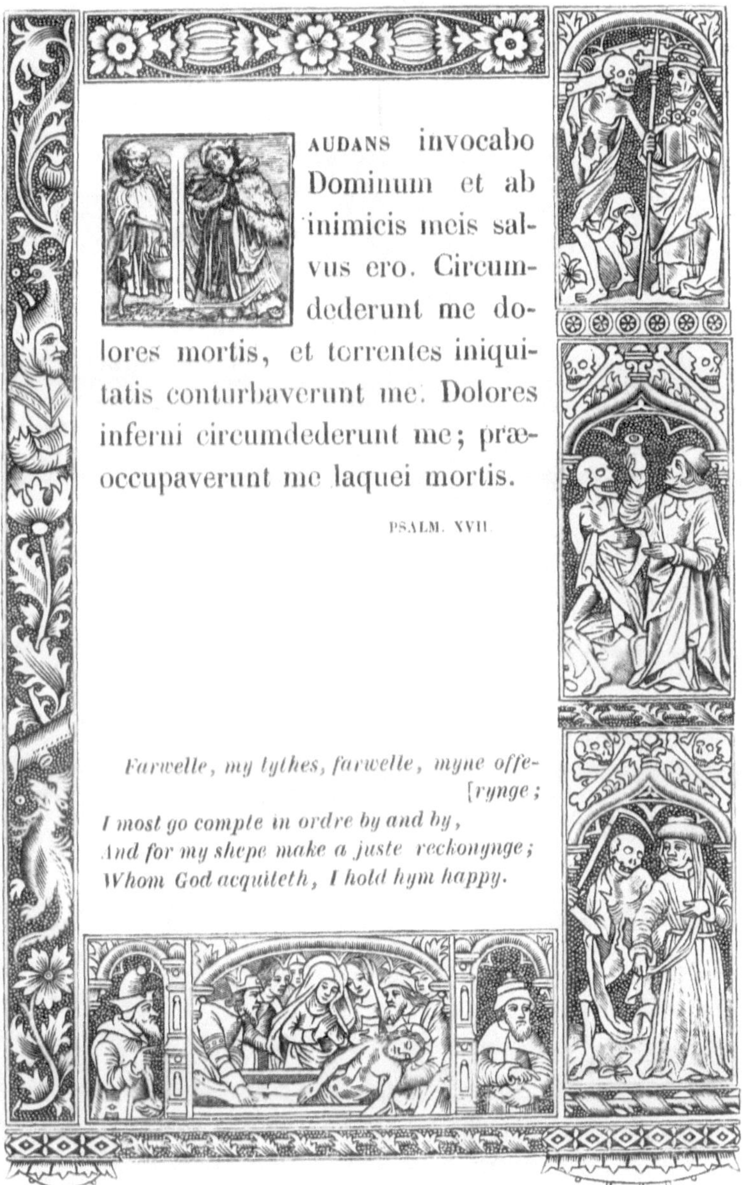

AUDANS invocabo Dominum et ab inimicis meis salvus ero. Circumdederunt me dolores mortis, et torrentes iniquitatis conturbaverunt me. Dolores inferni circumdederunt me; præoccupaverunt me laquei mortis.

PSALM. XVII.

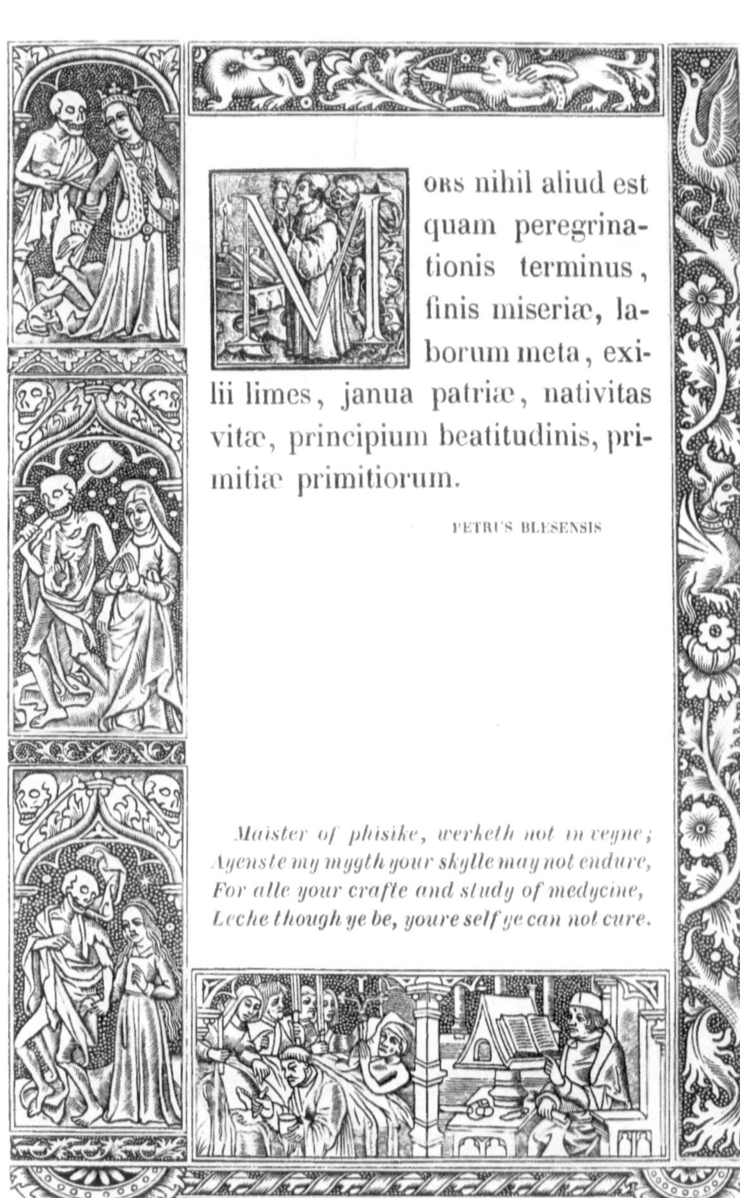

MORS nihil aliud est quam peregrinationis terminus, finis miseriæ, laborum meta, exilii limes, janua patriæ, nativitas vitæ, principium beatitudinis, primitiæ primitiorum.

PETRUS BLESENSIS

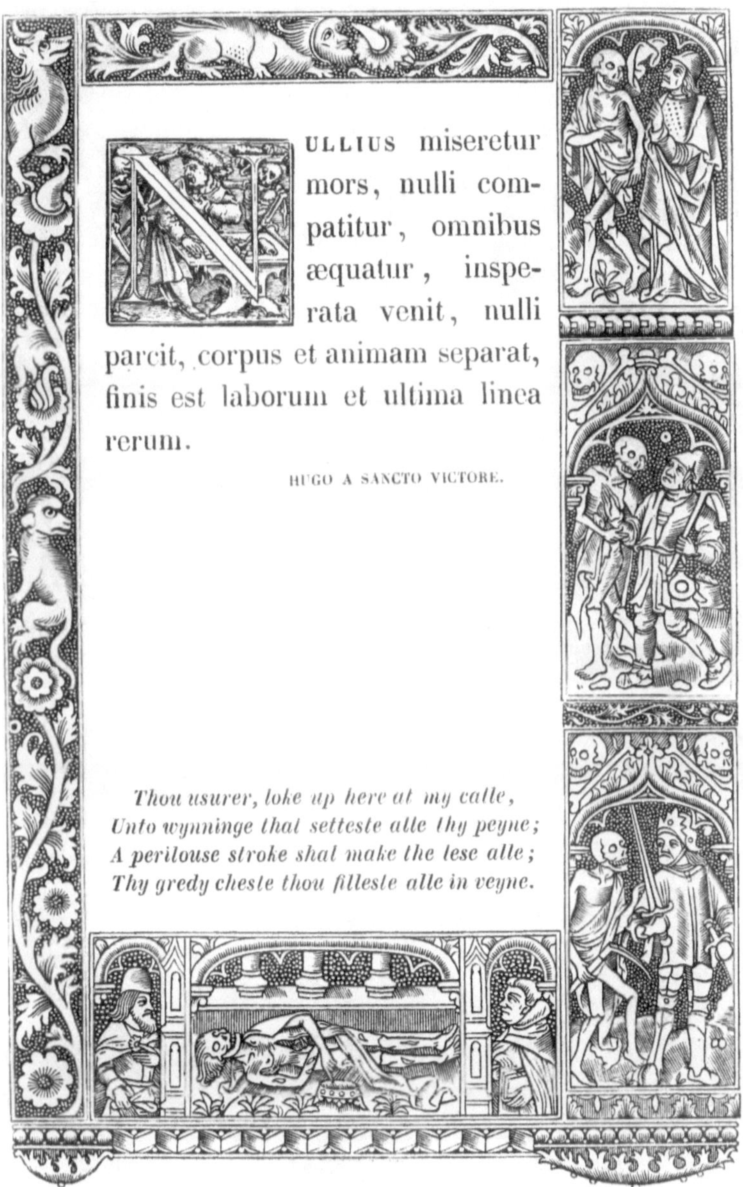

NULLIUS miseretur mors, nulli compatitur, omnibus æquatur, insperata venit, nulli parcit, corpus et animam separat, finis est laborum et ultima linea rerum.

HUGO A SANCTO VICTORE.

Thou usurer, loke up here at my calle,
Unto wynninge that setteste alle thy peyne;
A perilouse stroke shal make the lese alle;
Thy gredy cheste thou filleste alle in veyne.

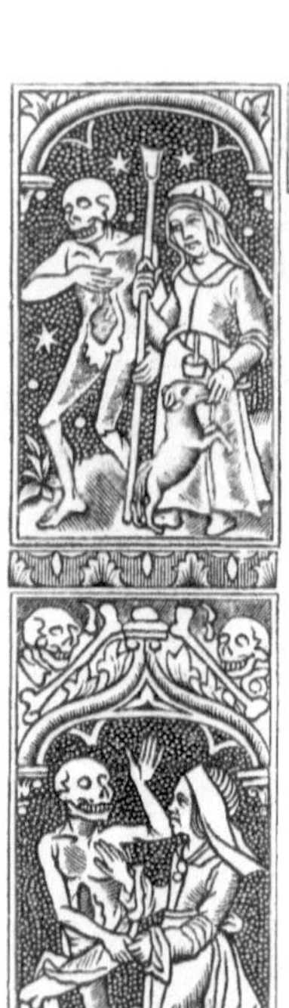

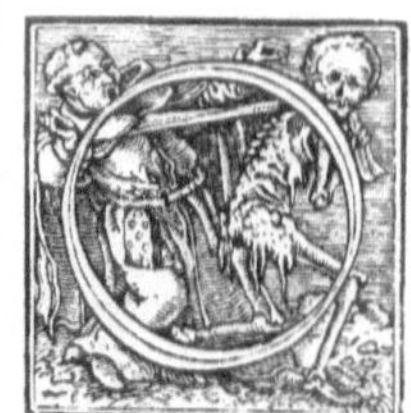

MISER homo, quo-
cumque te ver-
teris, incerta om-
nia, sola mors
certa. Pauper es,
incertum est an ditescas. Indo-
ctus, incertum est an crudiaris.
Imbecillis, incertum est an con-
valescas. Natus es; certum est quia
morieris, et in hoc ipso, quia
mors certa est, dies mortis incertus est, itaque hæc incerta.

S. AUGUSTINUS SUPER PSAL.

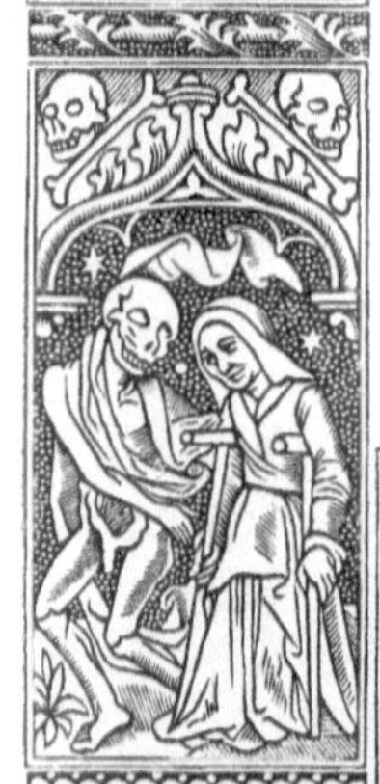

Sir corduler, to you myn hond is raught
To this daunce you to conveye and lede,
Which in your prechynge have ful ofte taught
How I am most gastfulle for to drede.

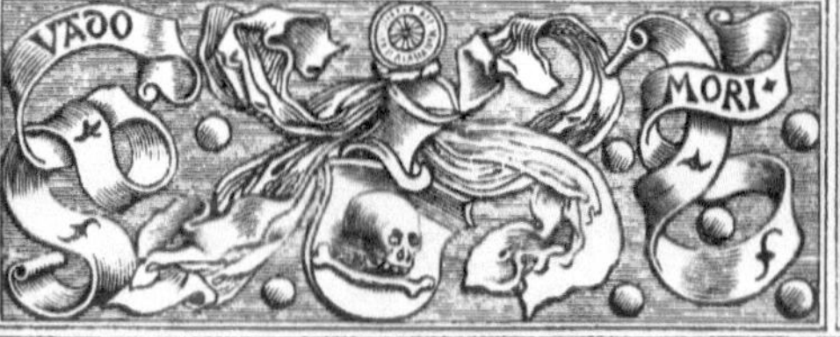

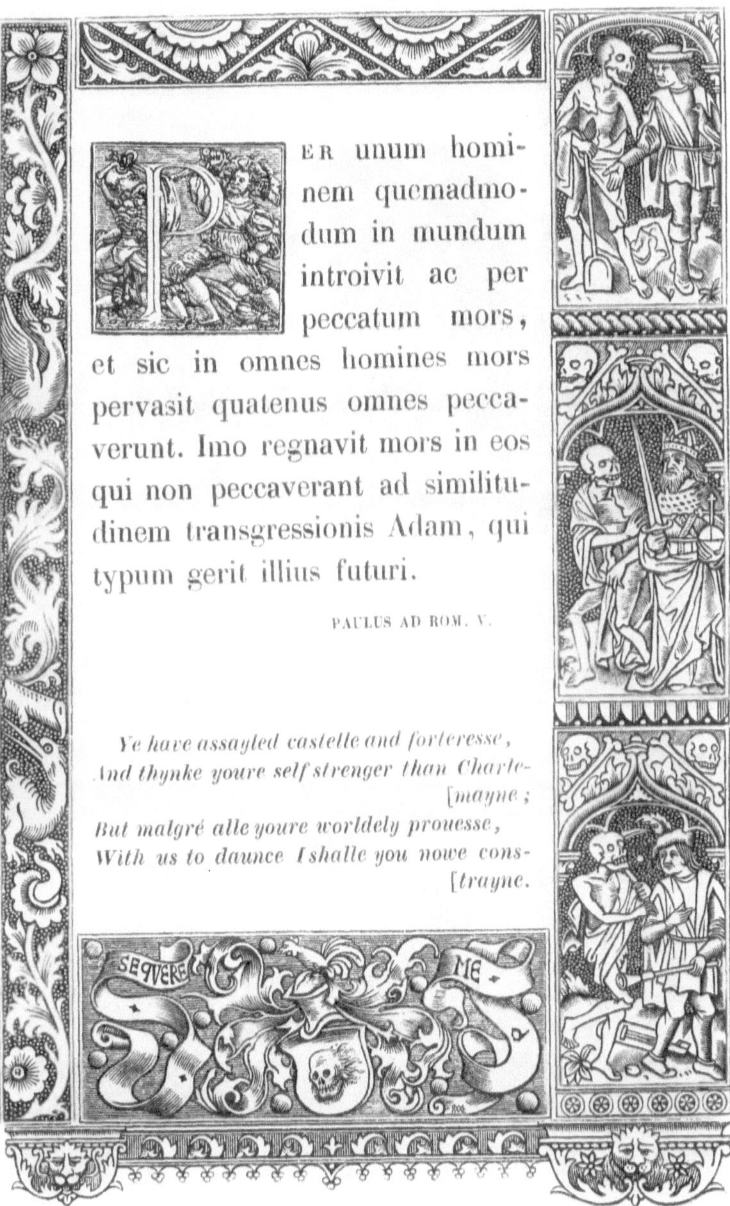

PER unum homi-
nem quemadmo-
dum in mundum
introivit ac per
peccatum mors,
et sic in omnes homines mors
pervasit quatenus omnes pecca-
verunt. Imo regnavit mors in eos
qui non peccaverant ad similitu-
dinem transgressionis Adam, qui
typum gerit illius futuri.

PAULUS AD ROM. V.

Ye have assayled castelle and forteresse,
And thynke youre self strenger than Charle-
[mayne;
But malgré alle youre worldely prouesse,
With us to daunce I shalle you nowe cons-
[trayne.

SEQVERE ME

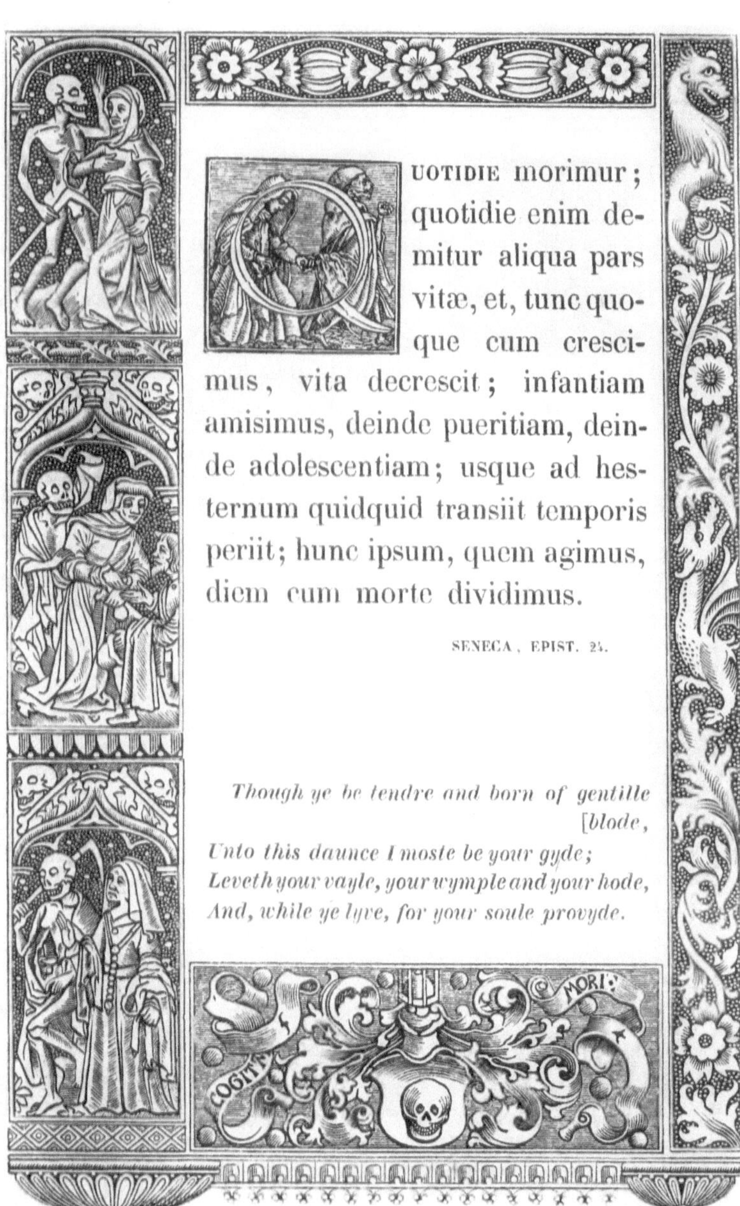

UOTIDIE morimur; quotidie enim demitur aliqua pars vitæ, et, tunc quoque cum crescimus, vita decrescit; infantiam amisimus, deinde pueritiam, deinde adolescentiam; usque ad hesternum quidquid transiit temporis periit; hunc ipsum, quem agimus, diem cum morte dividimus.

SENECA, EPIST. 24.

Though ye be tendre and born of gentille
        [blode,
Unto this daunce I moste be your gyde;
Leveth your vayle, your wymple and your hode,
And, while ye lyve, for your soule provyde.

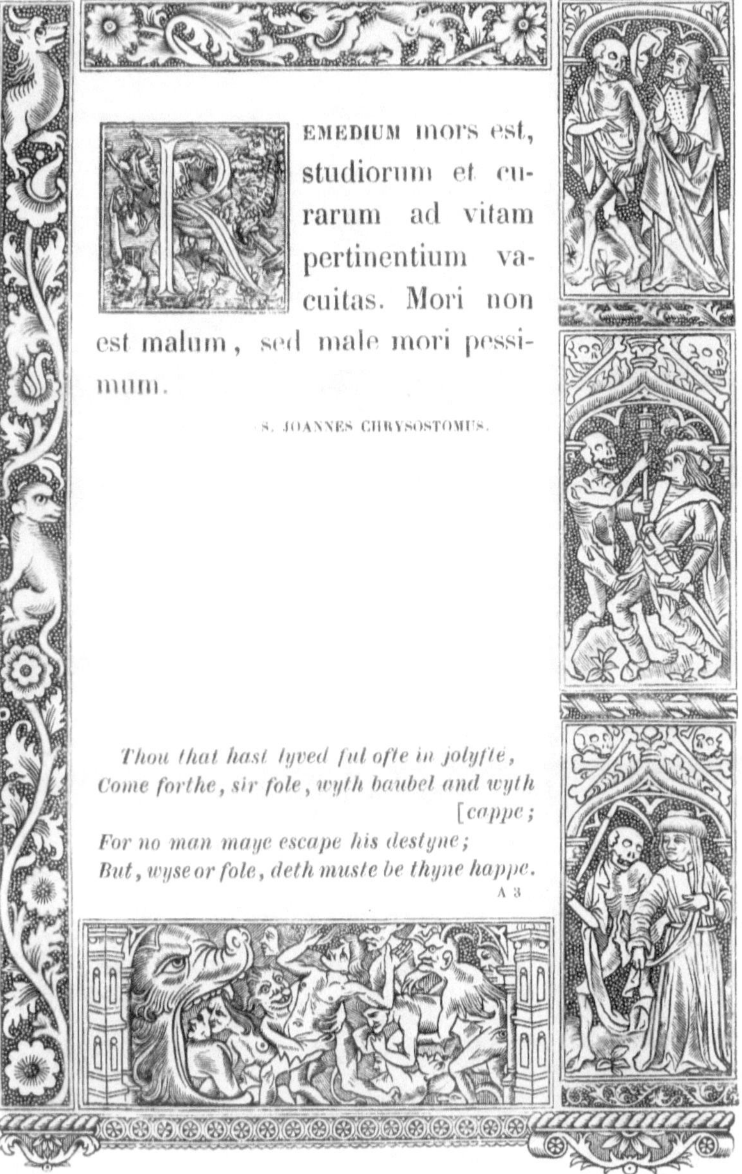

EMEDIUM mors est, studiorum et curarum ad vitam pertinentium vacuitas. Mori non est malum, sed male mori pessimum.

S. JOANNES CHRYSOSTOMUS.

A 3

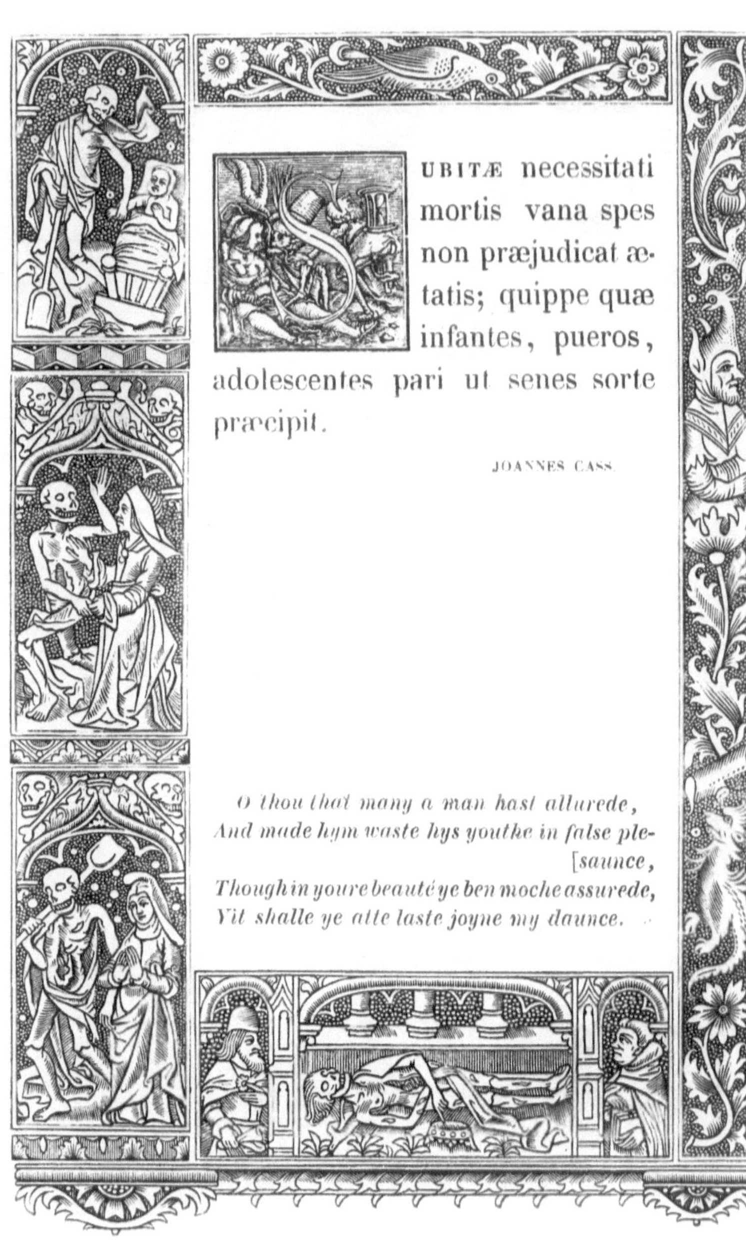

UBITÆ necessitati mortis vana spes non præjudicat ætatis; quippe quæ infantes, pueros, adolescentes pari ut senes sorte præcipit.

JOANNES CASS.

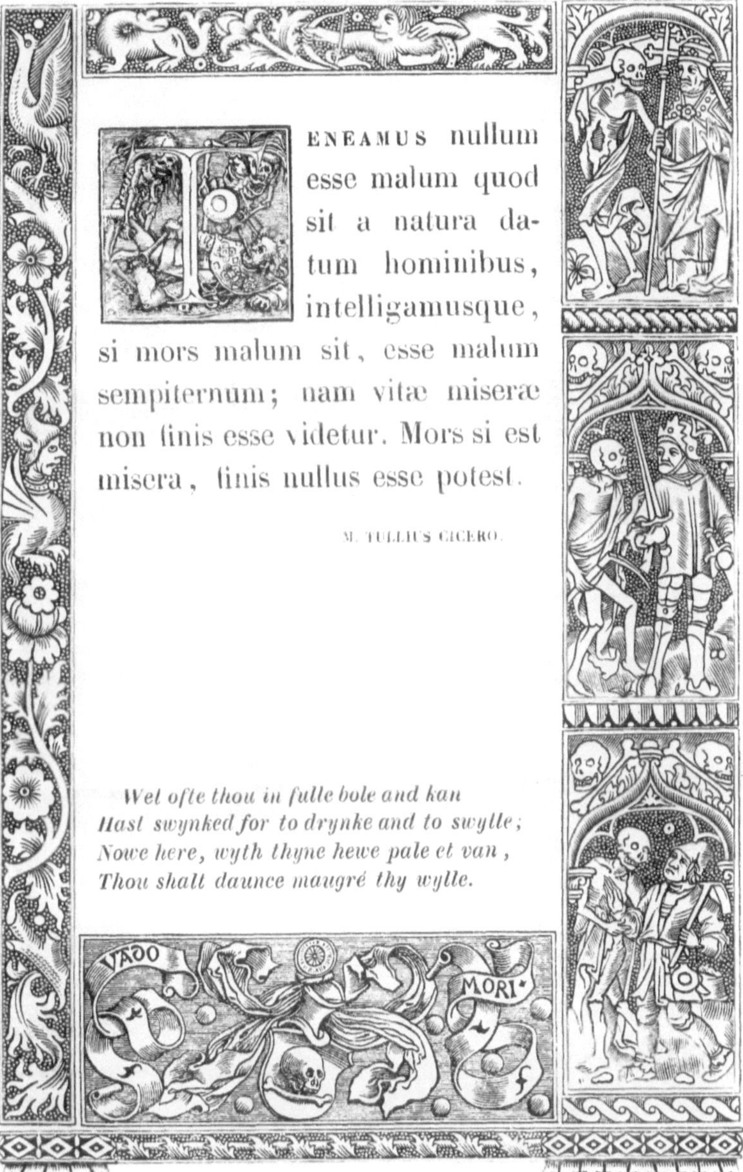

Teneamus nullum esse malum quod sit a natura datum hominibus, intelligamusque, si mors malum sit, esse malum sempiternum; nam vitæ miseræ non finis esse videtur. Mors si est misera, finis nullus esse potest.

M. TULLIUS CICERO.

Wel ofte thou in fulle bole and kan
Hast swynked for to drynke and to swylle;
Nowe here, wyth thyne hewe pale et van,
Thou shall daunce maugré thy wylle.

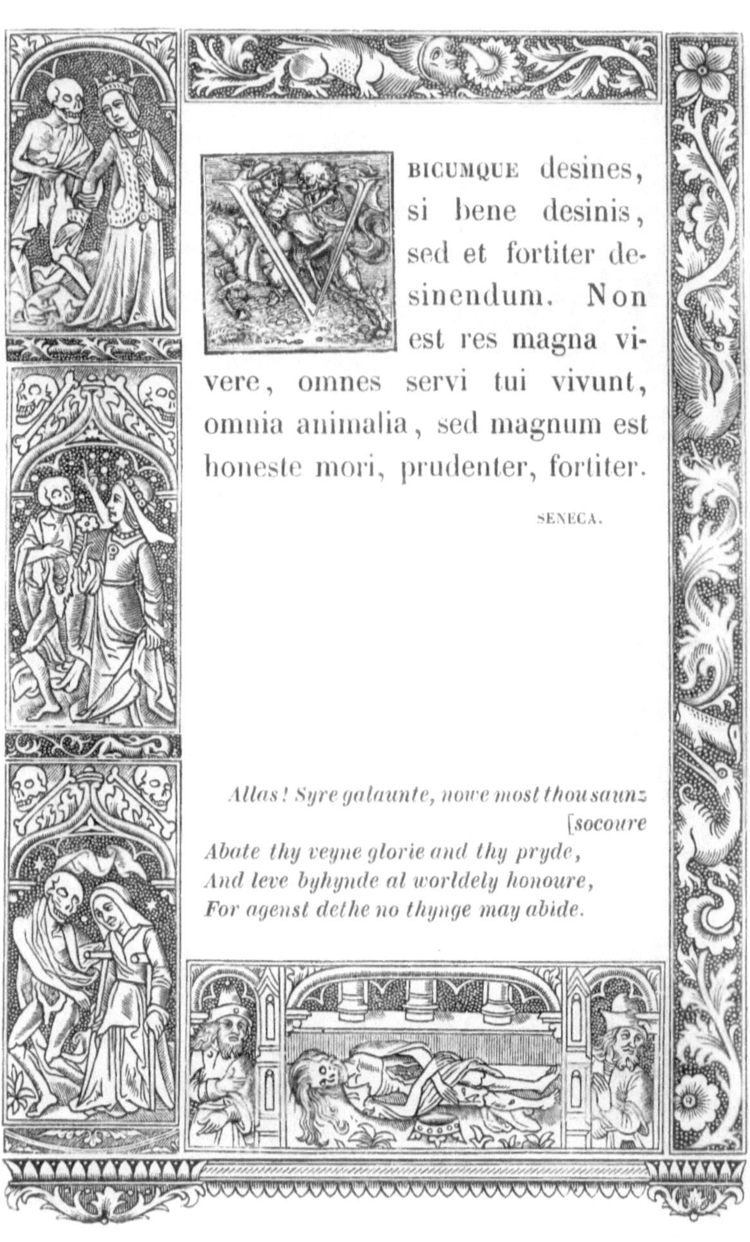

BICUMQUE desines, si bene desinis, sed et fortiter desinendum. Non est res magna vivere, omnes servi tui vivunt, omnia animalia, sed magnum est honeste mori, prudenter, fortiter.

SENECA.

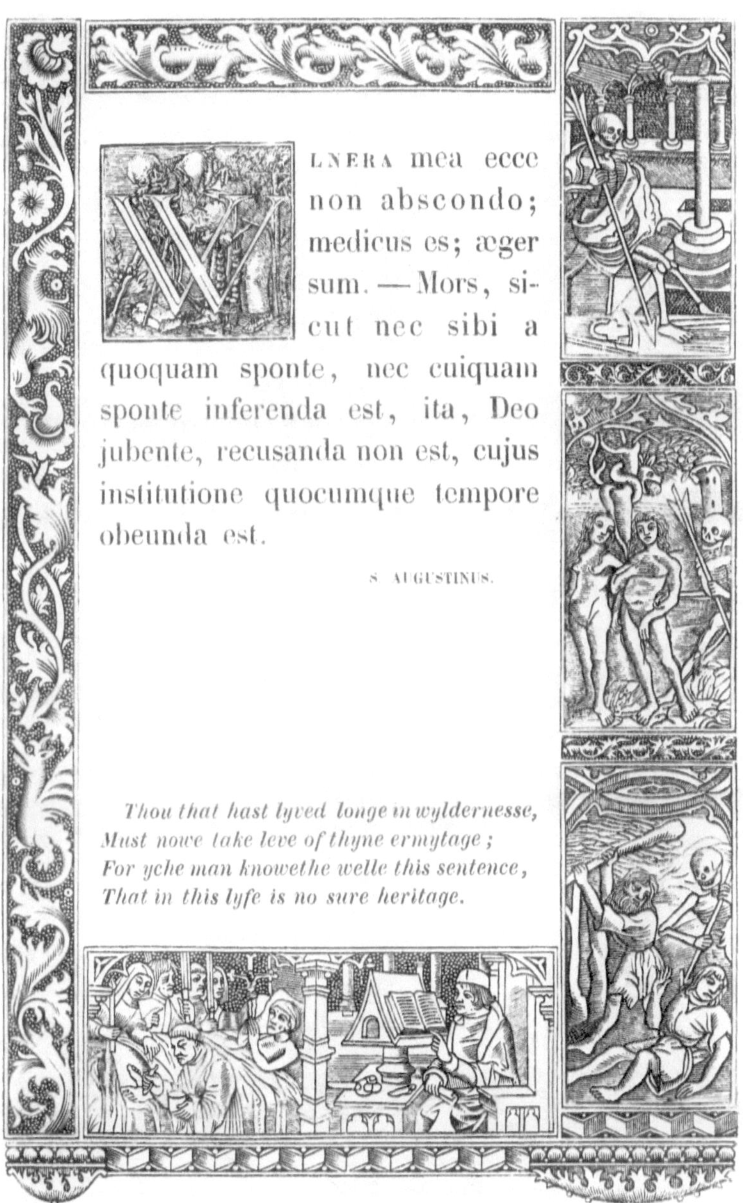

VLNERA mea ecce non abscondo; medicus es; æger sum. — Mors, sicut nec sibi a quoquam sponte, nec cuiquam sponte inferenda est, ita, Deo jubente, recusanda non est, cujus institutione quocumque tempore obeunda est.

S. AUGUSTINUS.

Thou that hast lyved longe in wyldernesse,
Must nowe take leve of thyne ermytage;
For yche man knowethe welle this sentence,
That in this lyfe is no sure heritage.

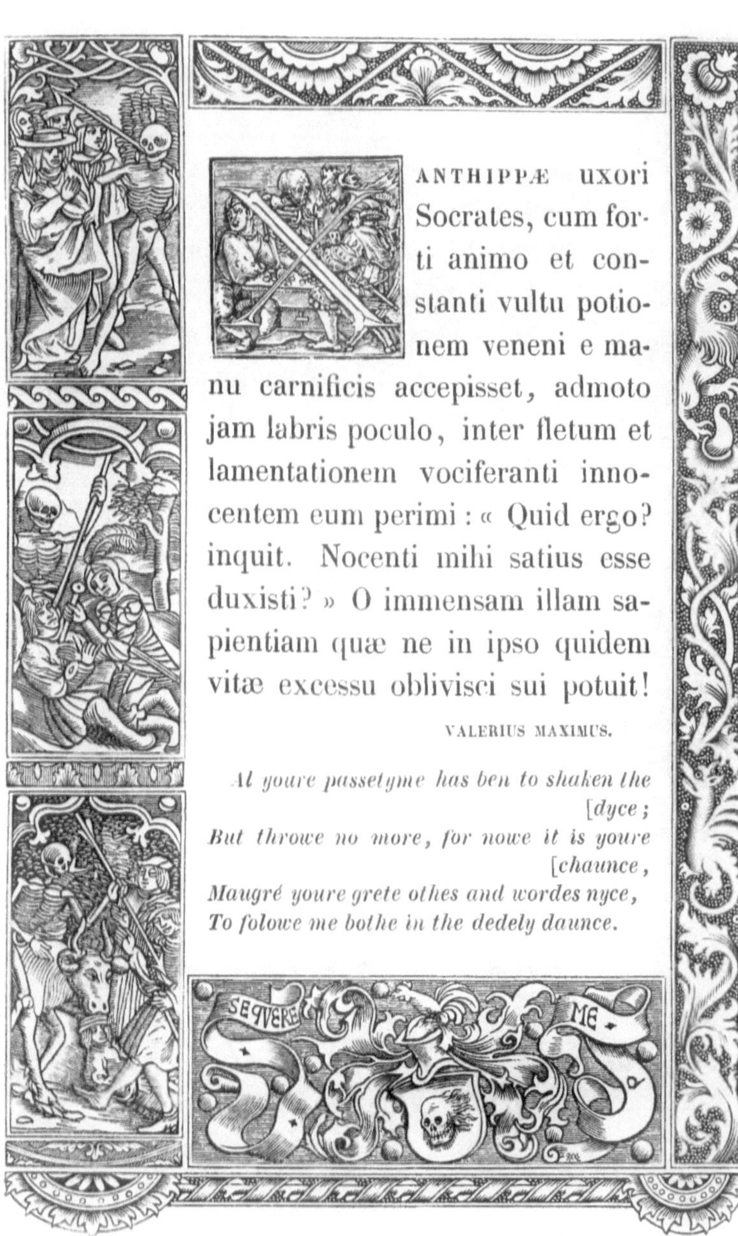

ANTHIPPÆ uxori Socrates, cum forti animo et constanti vultu potionem veneni e manu carnificis accepisset, admoto jam labris poculo, inter fletum et lamentationem vociferanti innocentem eum perimi : « Quid ergo? inquit. Nocenti mihi satius esse duxisti? » O immensam illam sapientiam quæ ne in ipso quidem vitæ excessu oblivisci sui potuit!

VALERIUS MAXIMUS.

Al youre passetyme has ben to shaken the
[dyce ;
But throwe no more, for nowe it is youre
[chaunce,
Maugré youre grete othes and wordes nyce,
To folowe me bothe in the dedely daunce.

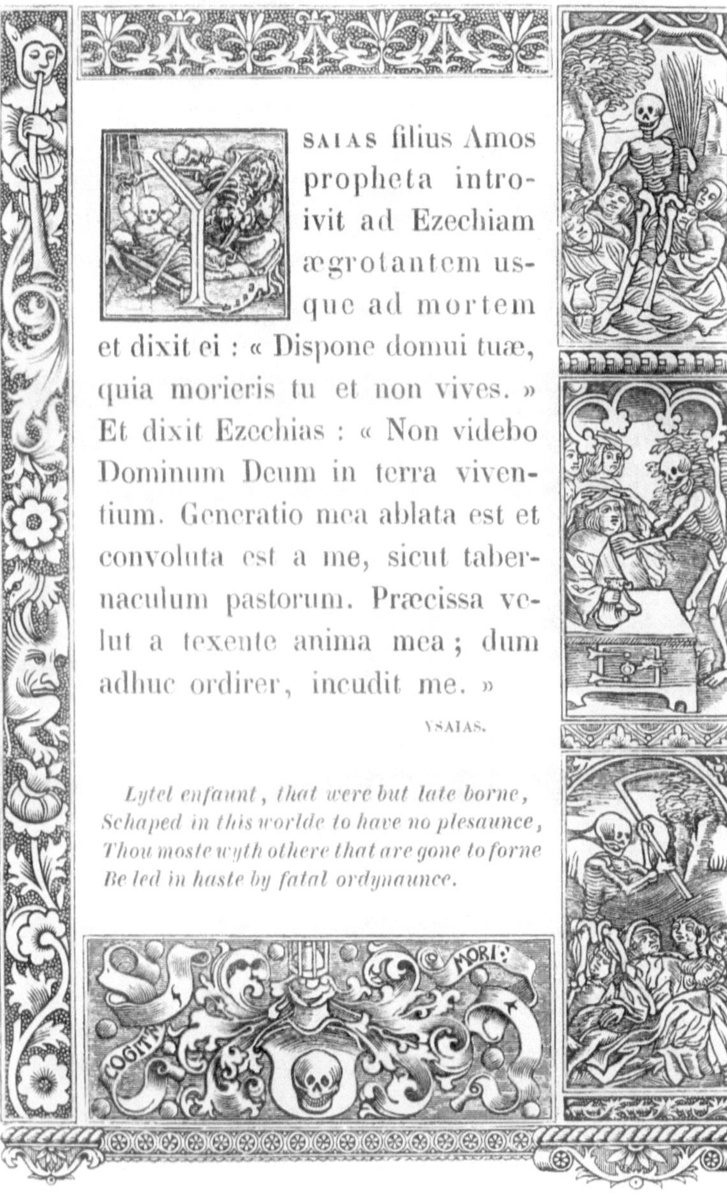

SAIAS filius Amos propheta introivit ad Ezechiam ægrotantem usque ad mortem
et dixit ei : « Dispone domui tuæ,
quia morieris tu et non vives. »
Et dixit Ezechias : « Non videbo
Dominum Deum in terra viven-
tium. Generatio mea ablata est et
convoluta est a me, sicut taber-
naculum pastorum. Præcissa ve-
lut a texente anima mea ; dum
adhuc ordirer, incudit me. »

YSAIAS.

Lytel enfaunt, that were but late borne,
Schaped in this worlde to have no plesaunce,
Thou moste wyth othere that are gone to forne
Be led in haste by fatal ordynaunce.

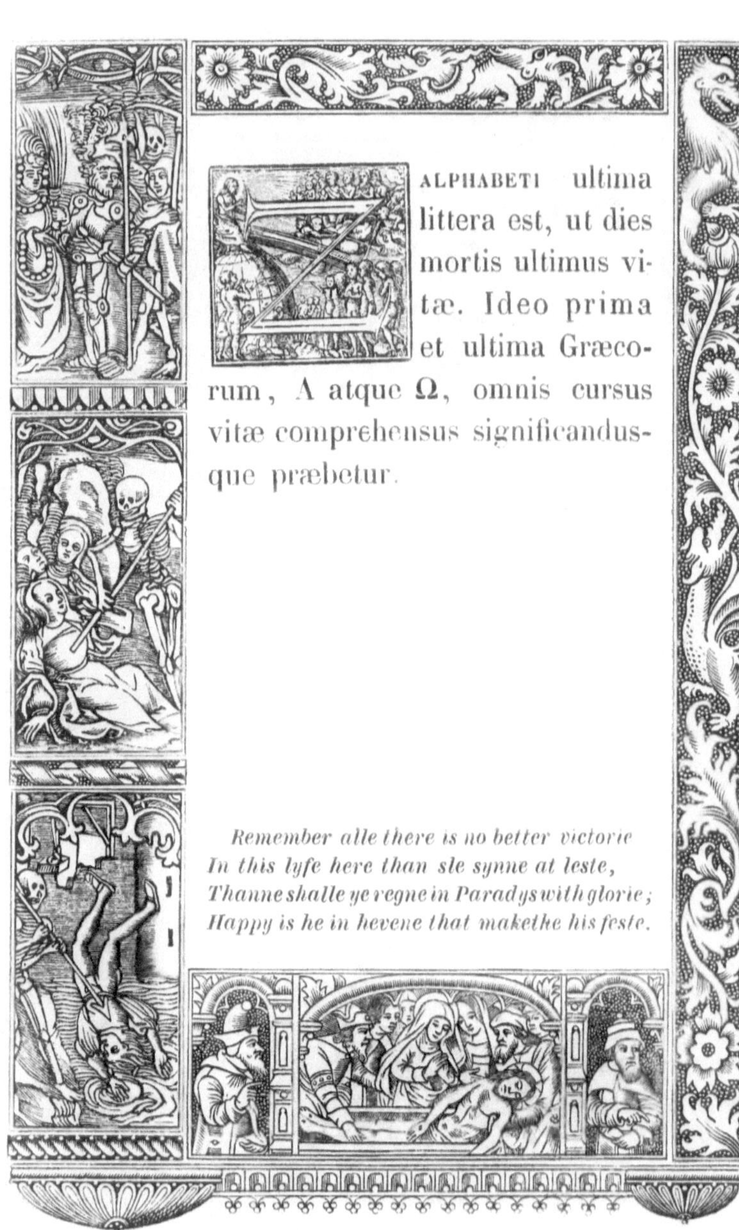

ALPHABETI ultima littera est, ut dies mortis ultimus vitæ. Ideo prima et ultima Græcorum, A atque Ω, omnis cursus vitæ comprehensus significandusque præbetur.

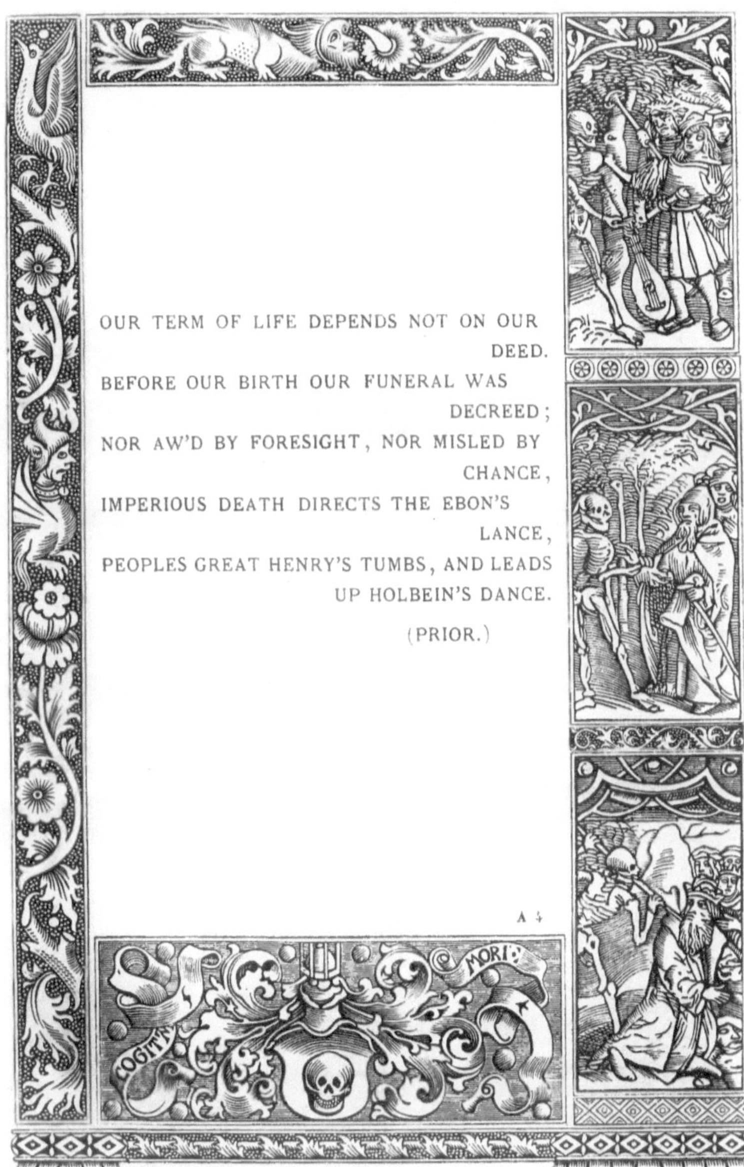

OUR TERM OF LIFE DEPENDS NOT ON OUR
DEED.
BEFORE OUR BIRTH OUR FUNERAL WAS
DECREED;
NOR AW'D BY FORESIGHT, NOR MISLED BY
CHANCE,
IMPERIOUS DEATH DIRECTS THE EBON'S
LANCE,
PEOPLES GREAT HENRY'S TUMBS, AND LEADS
UP HOLBEIN'S DANCE.

(PRIOR.)

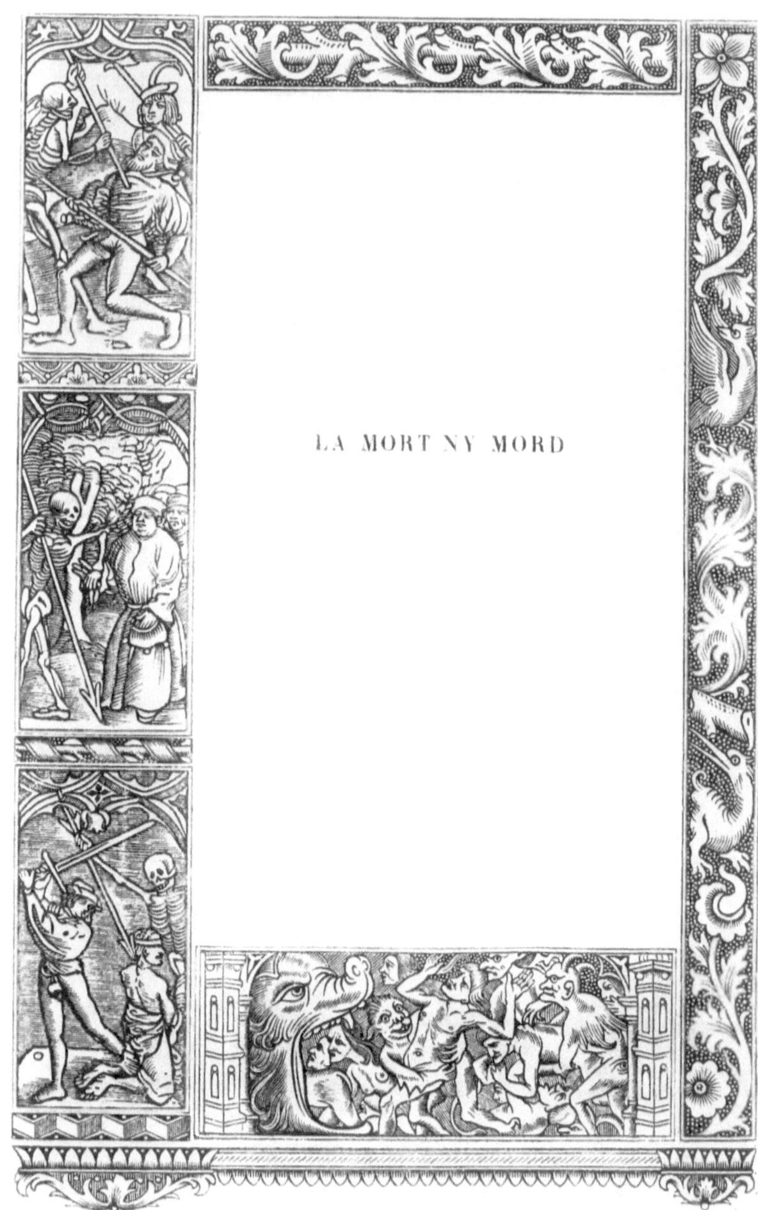

LA MORT NY MORD

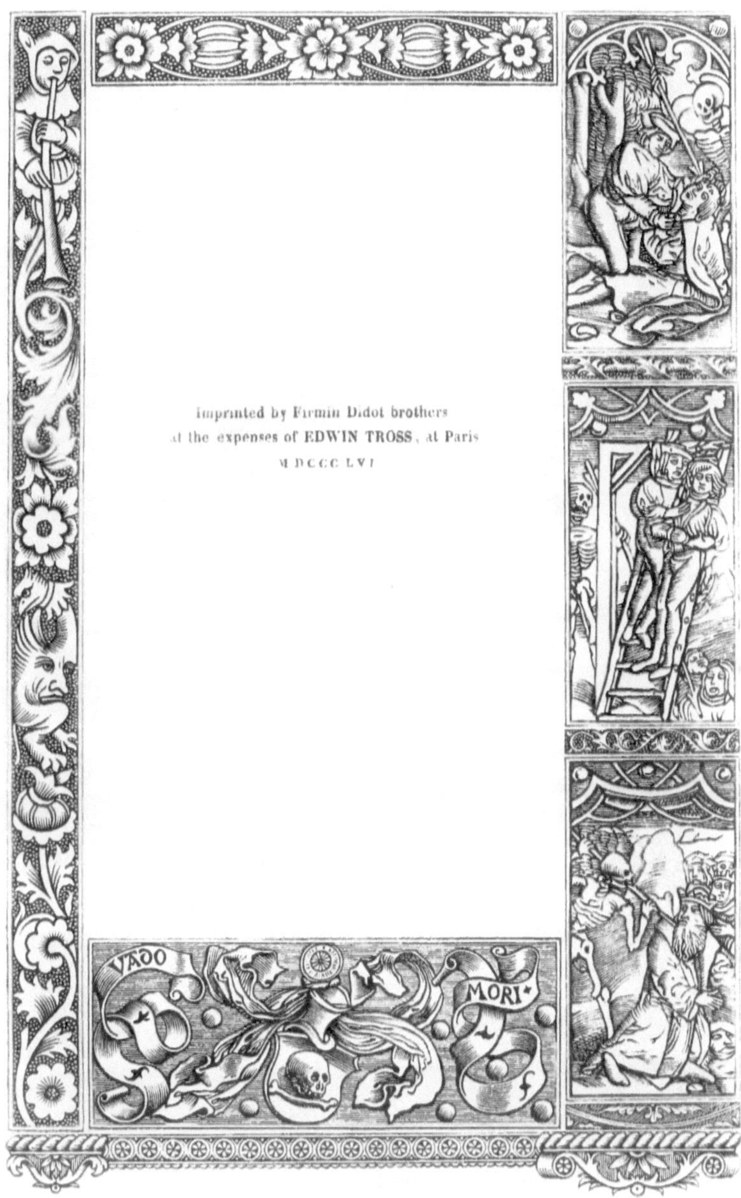

Imprinted by Firmin Didot brothers
at the expenses of EDWIN TROSS, at Paris
M DCCC LVI

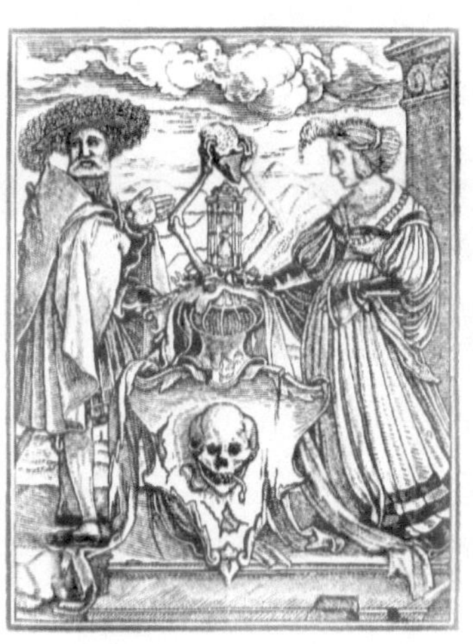

A Closer Look At
The Alphabet of Death

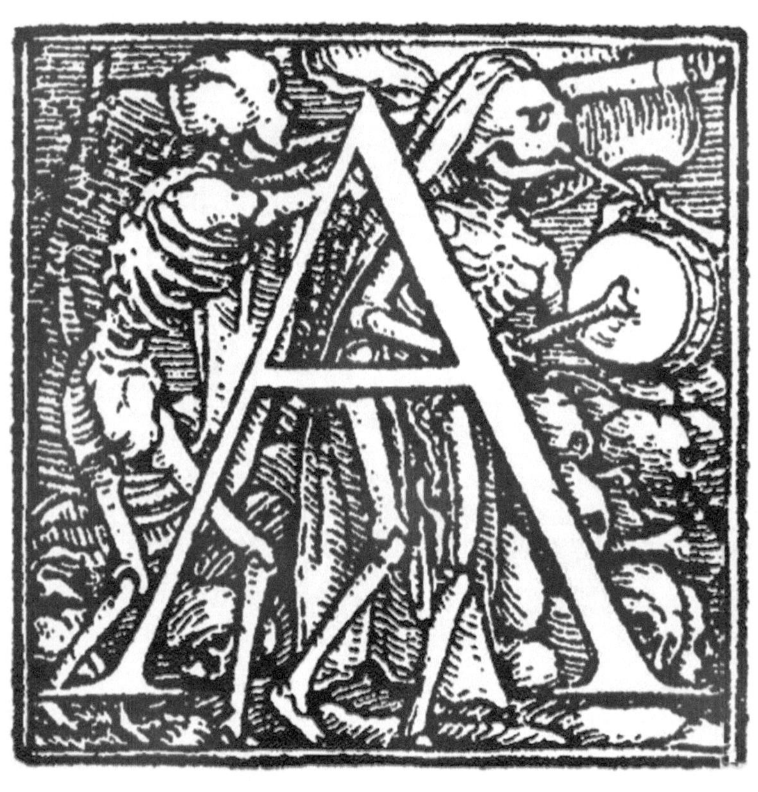

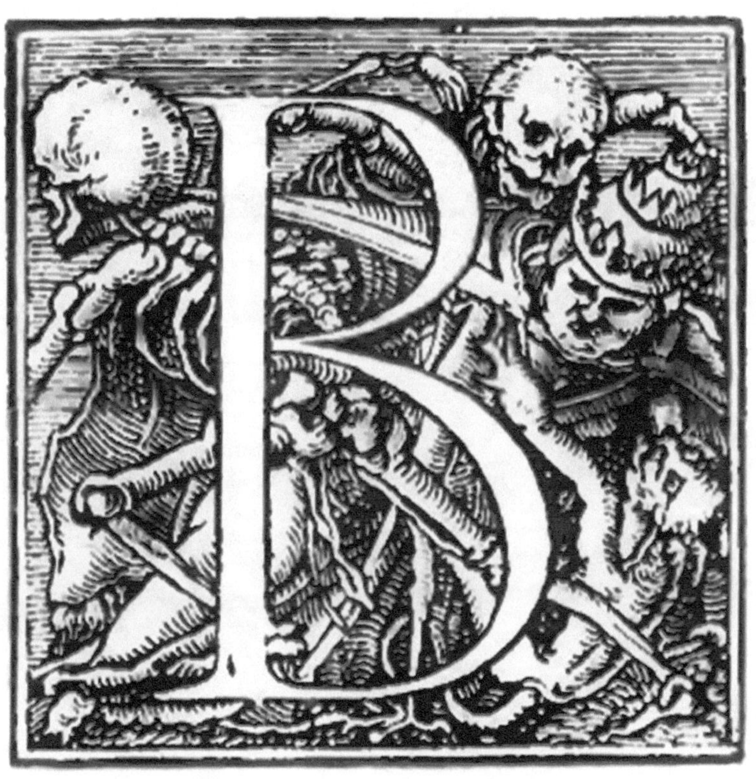

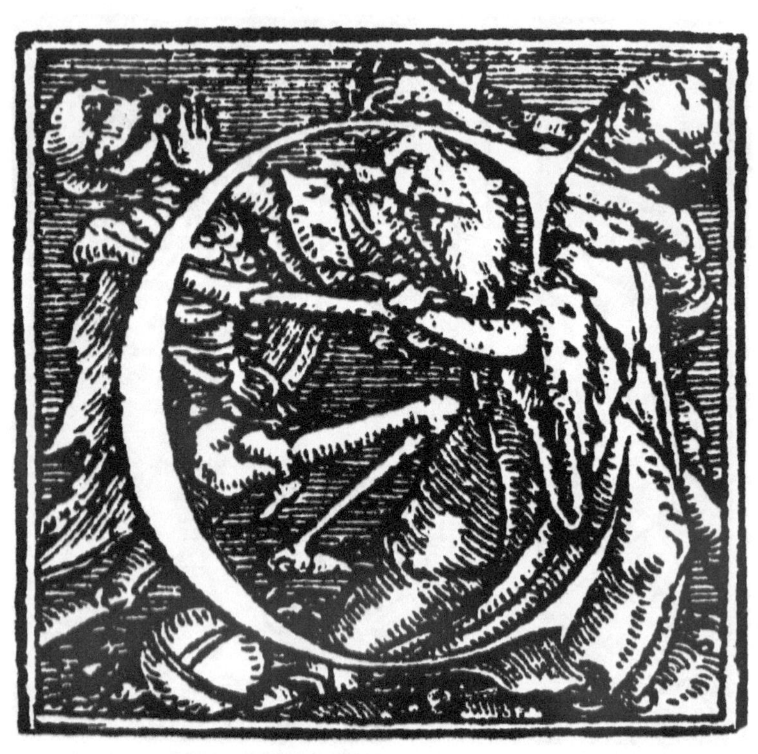

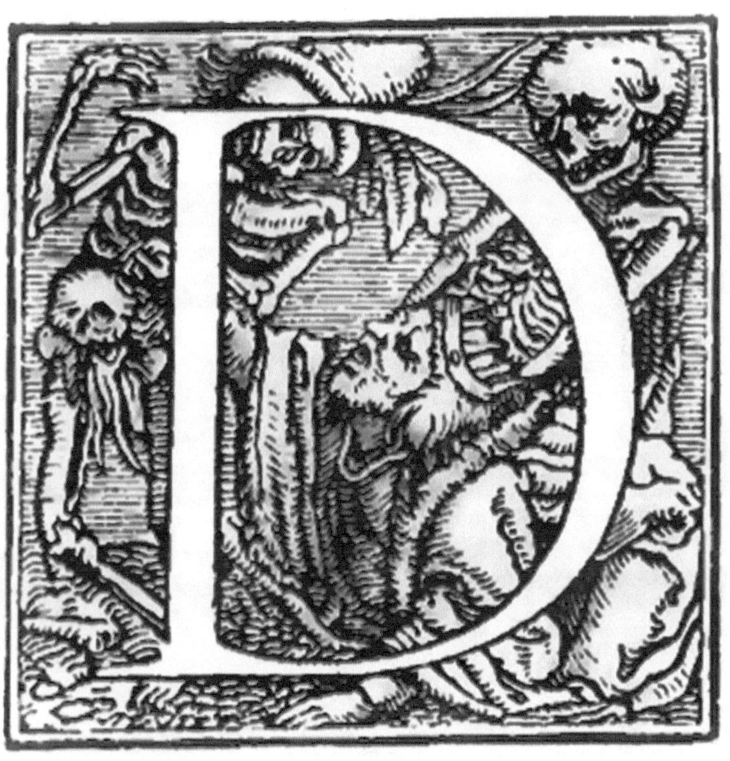

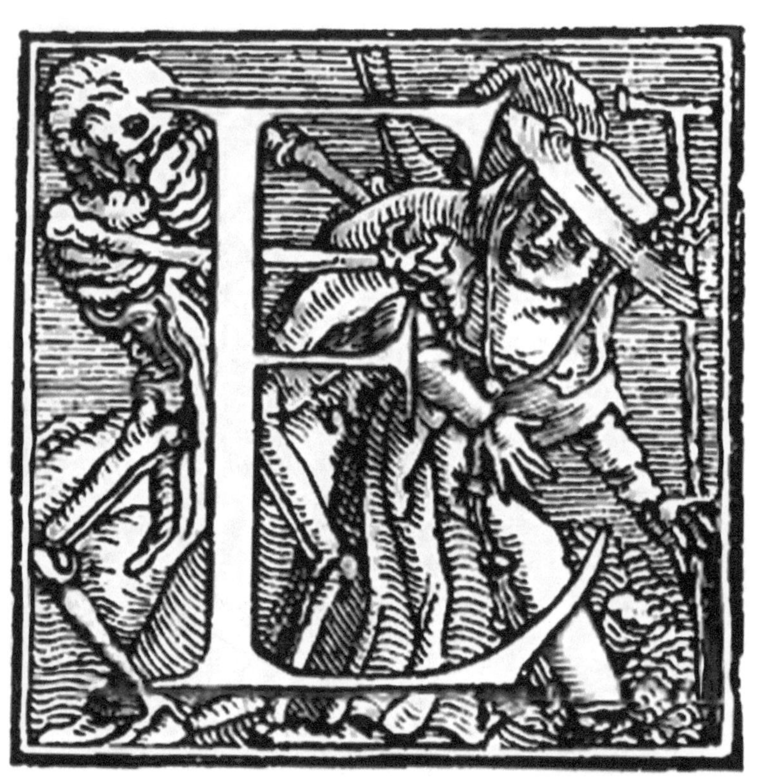

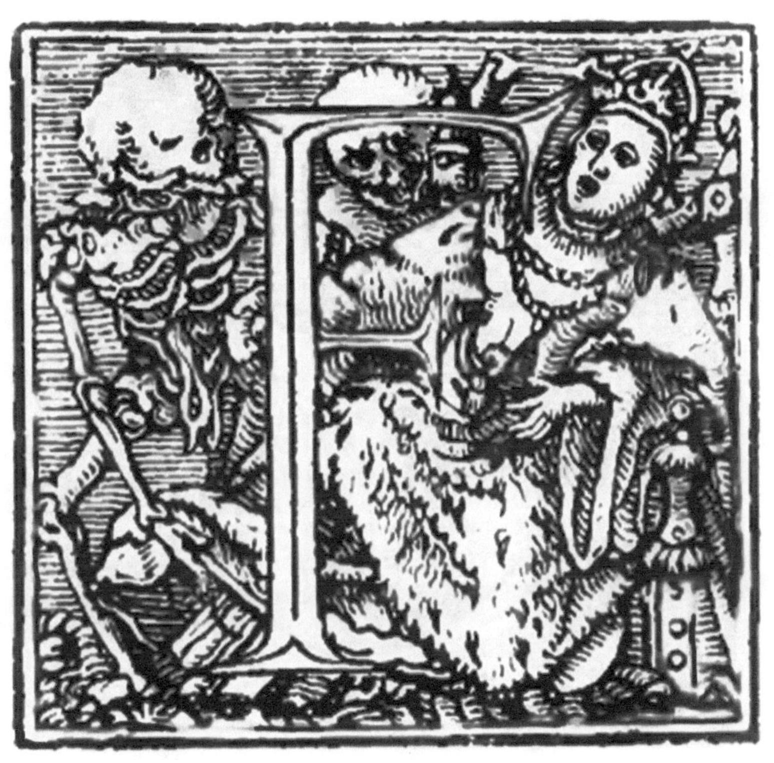

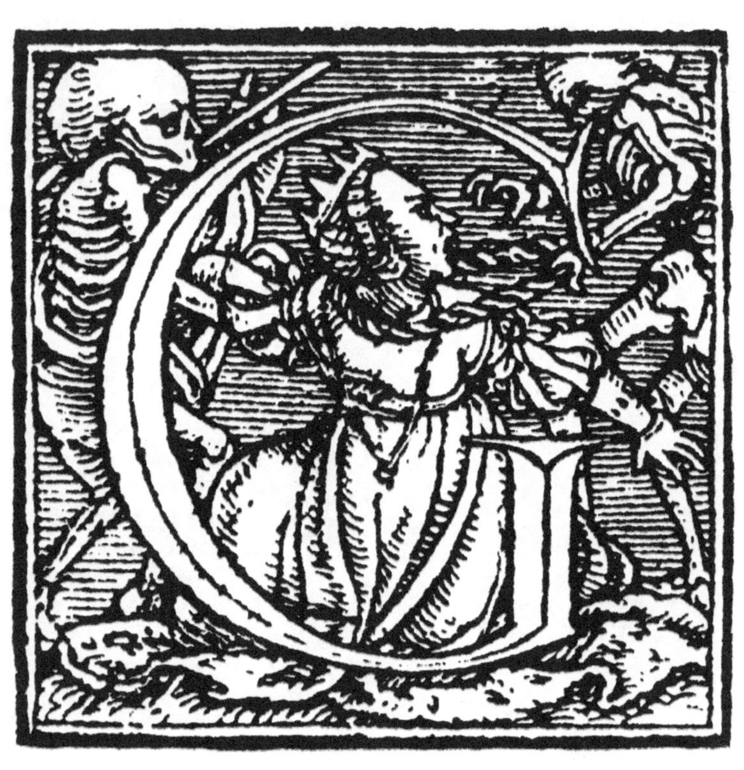

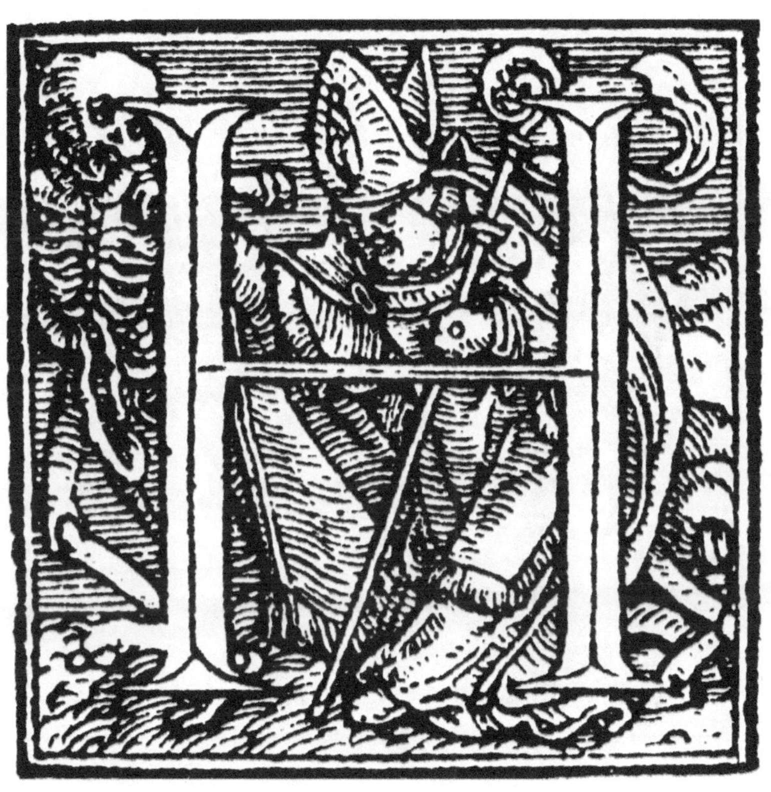

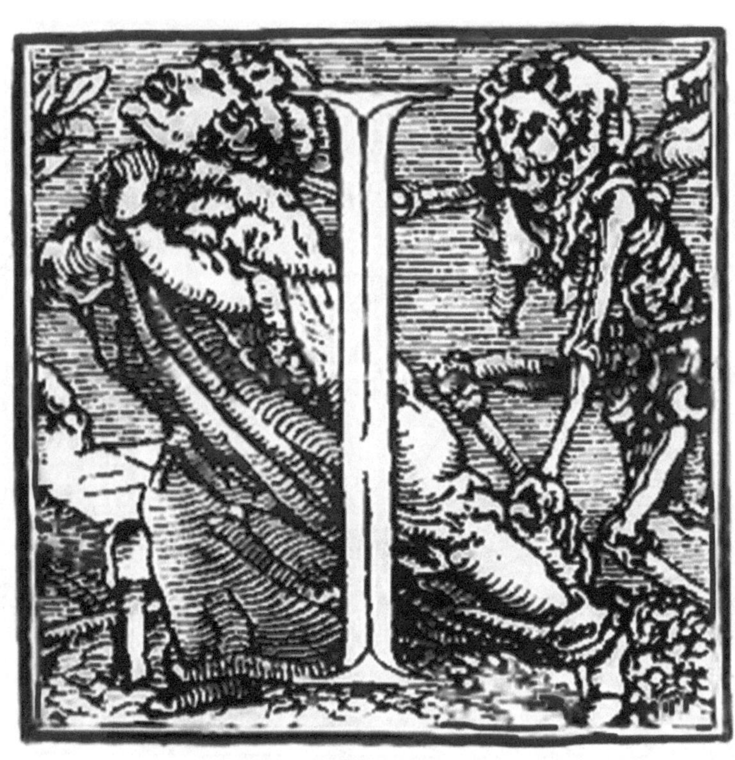

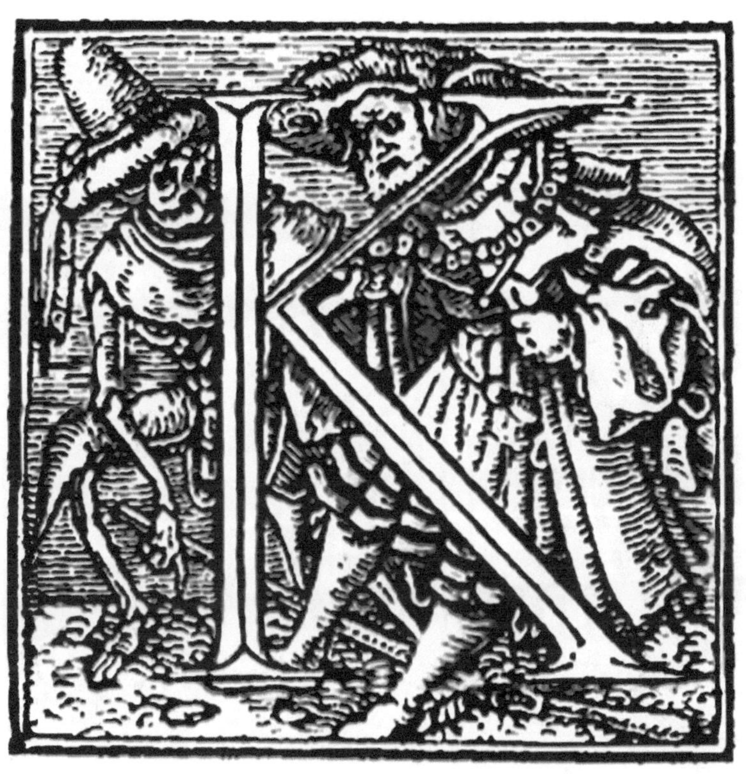

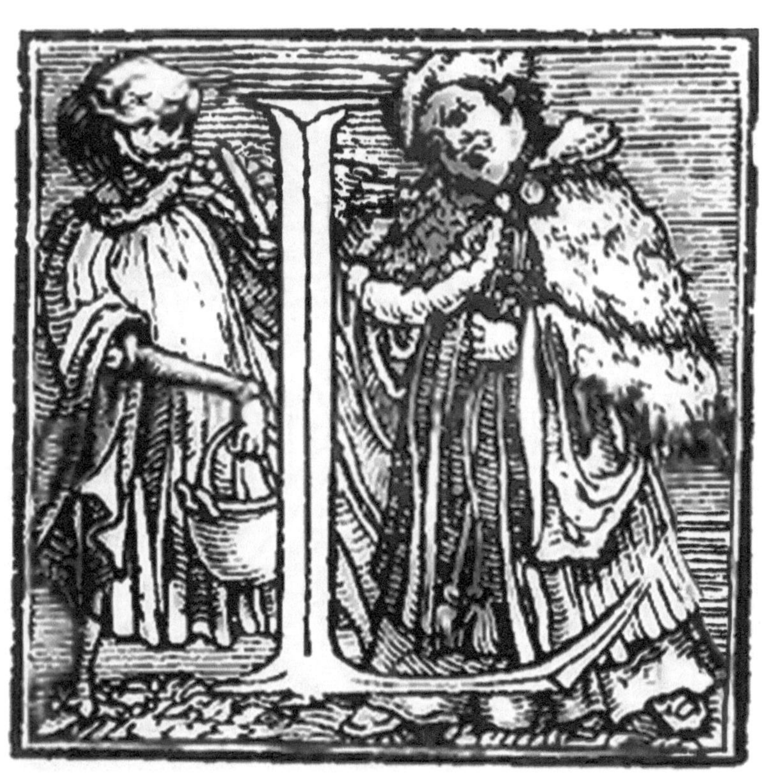

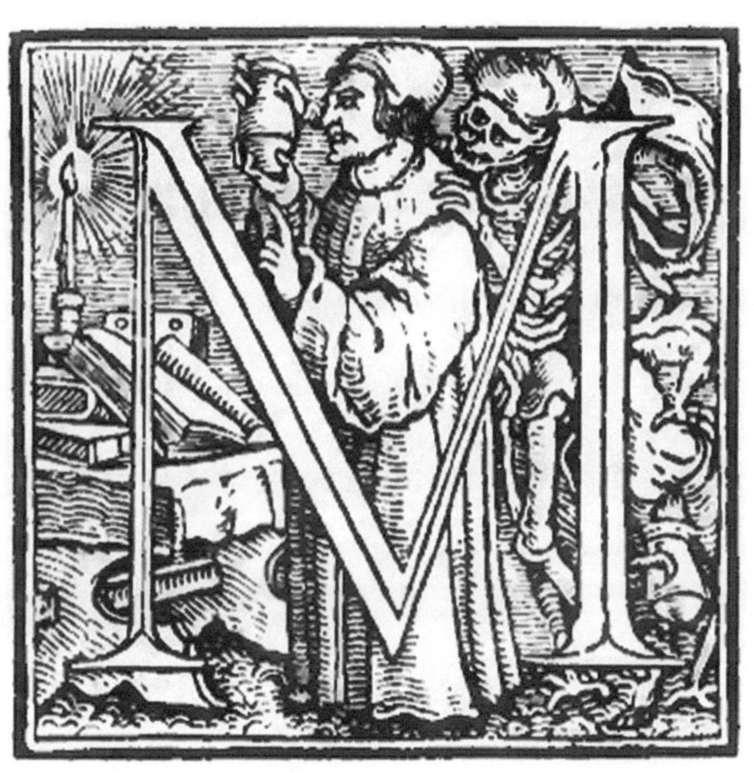

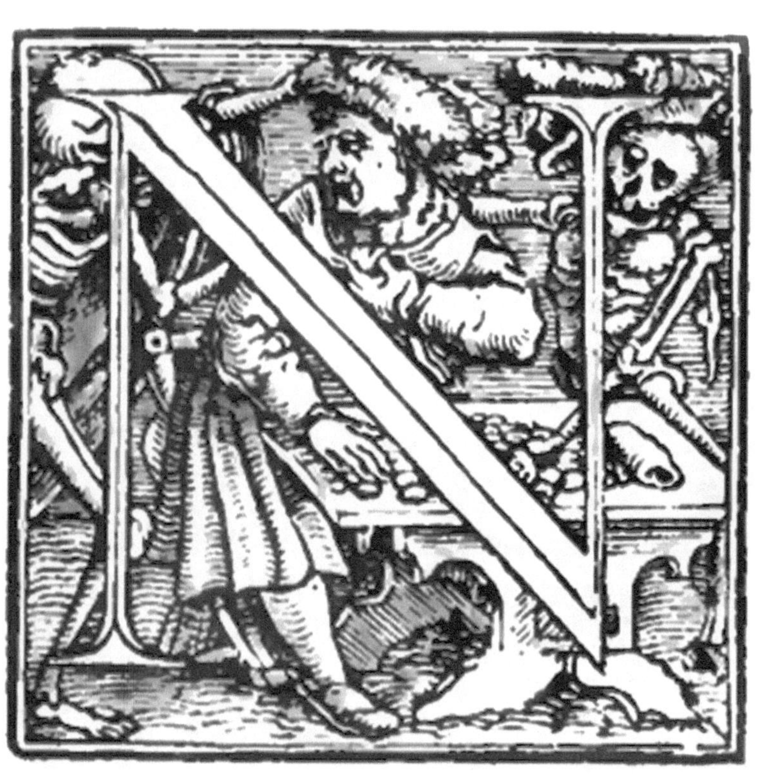

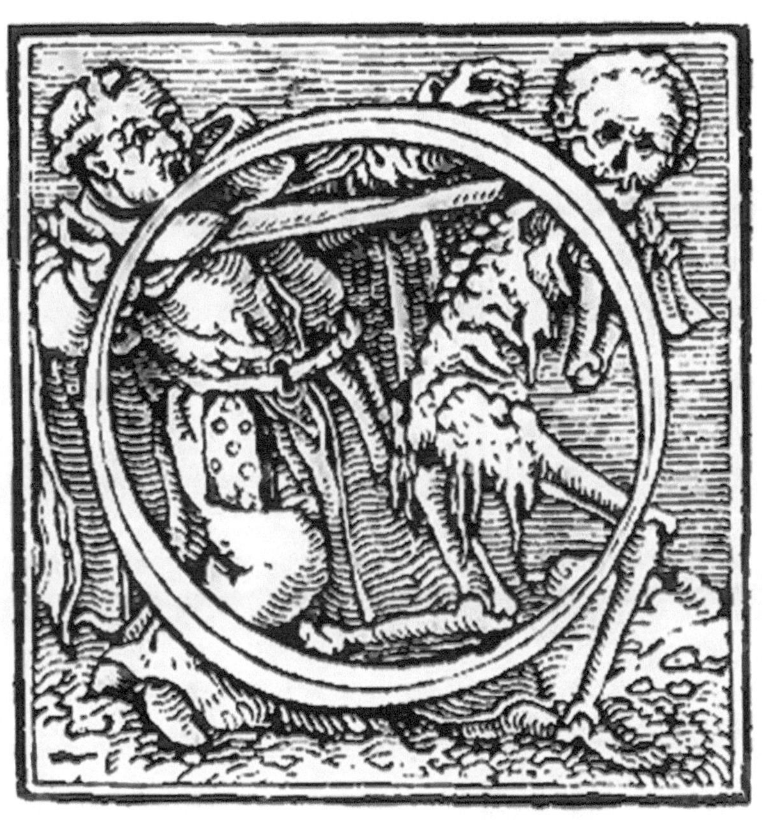

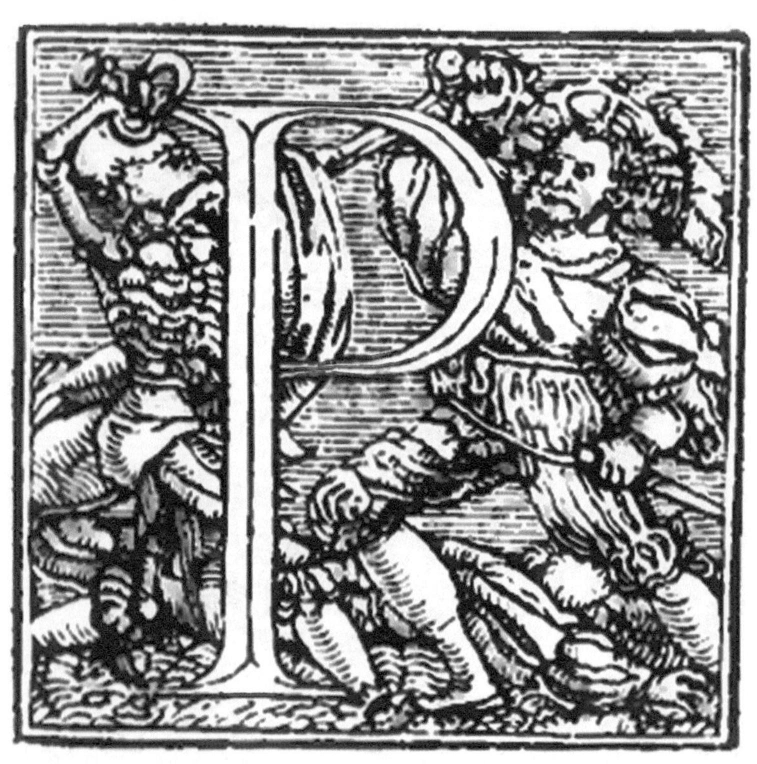

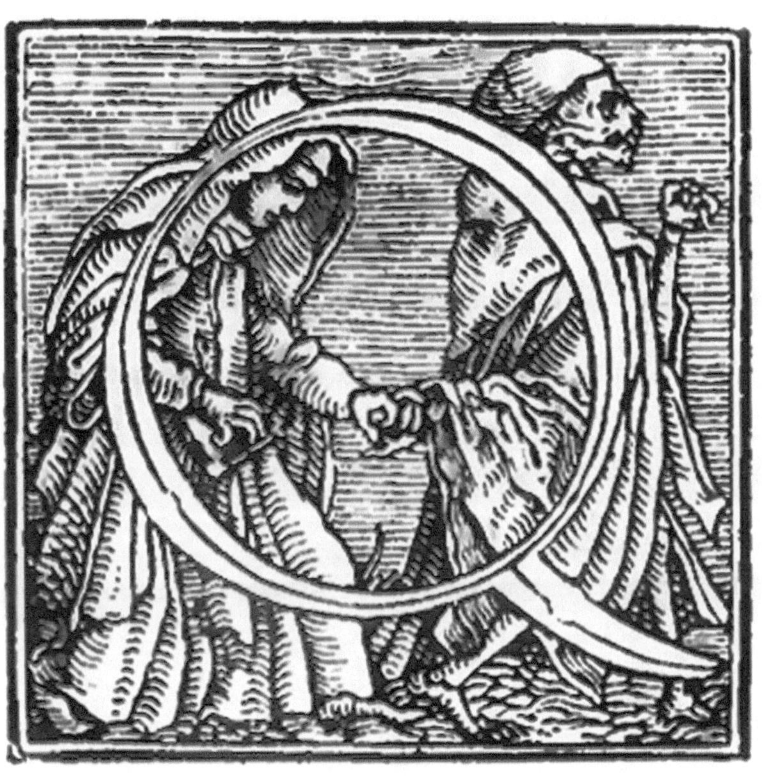

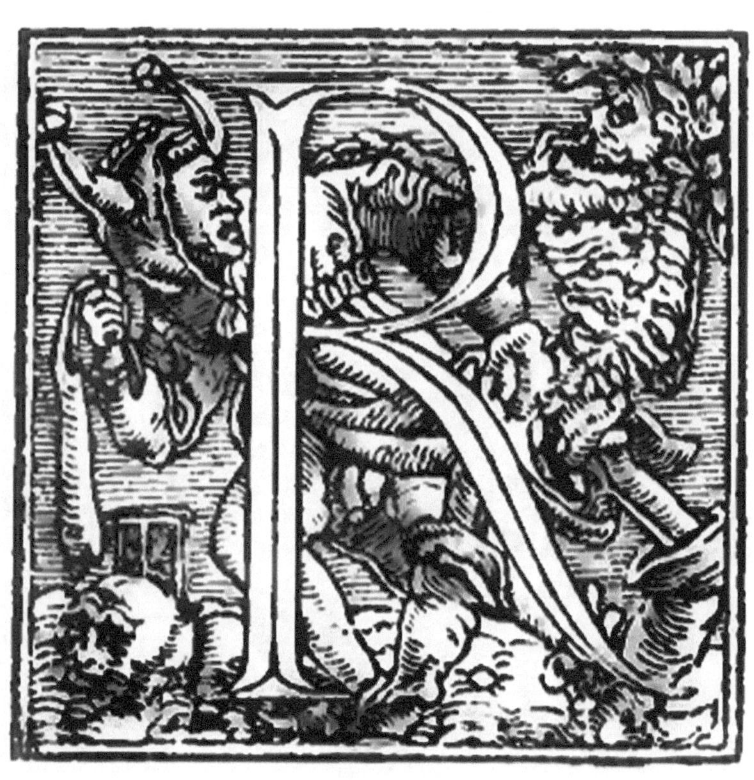

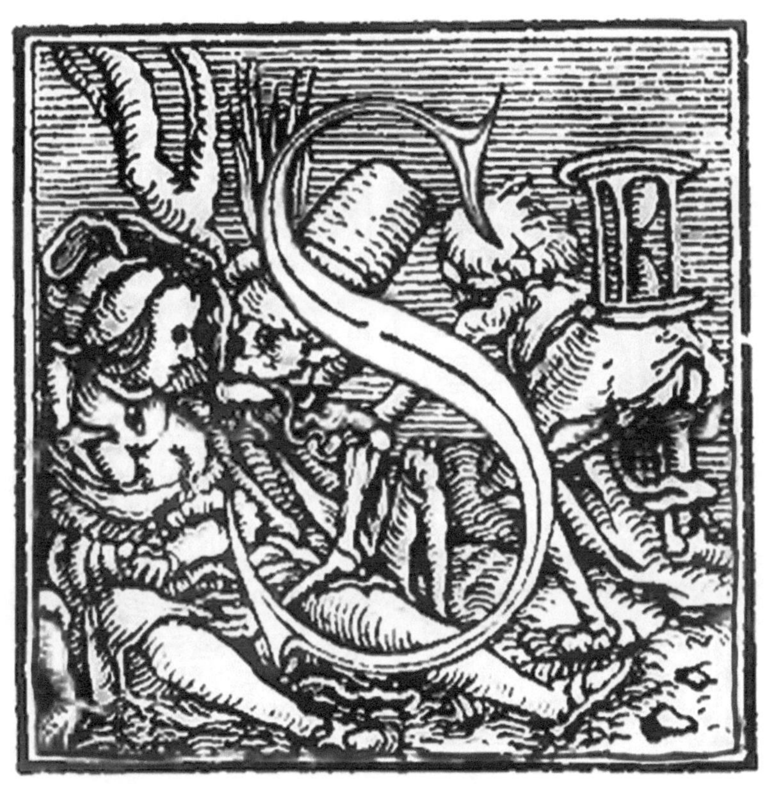

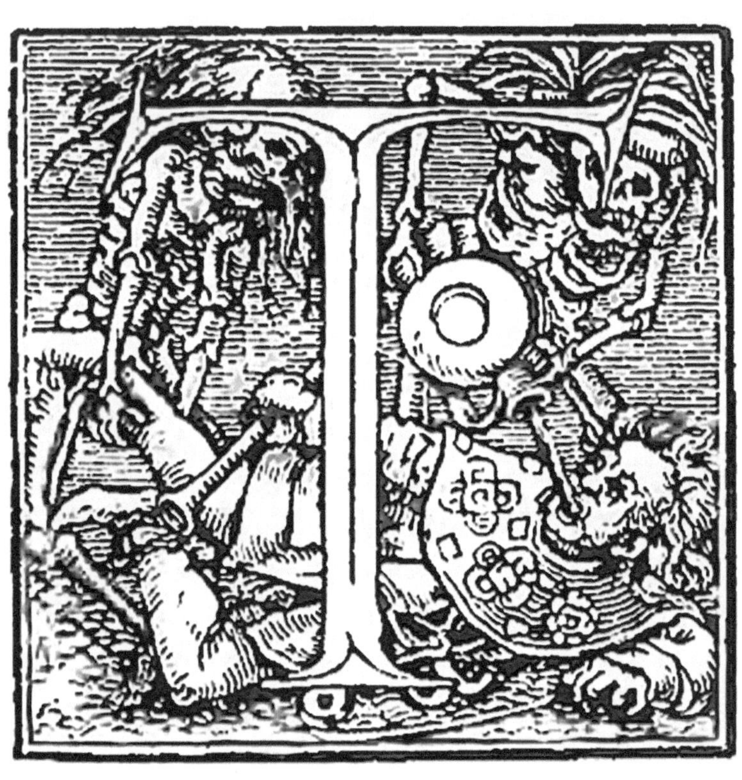

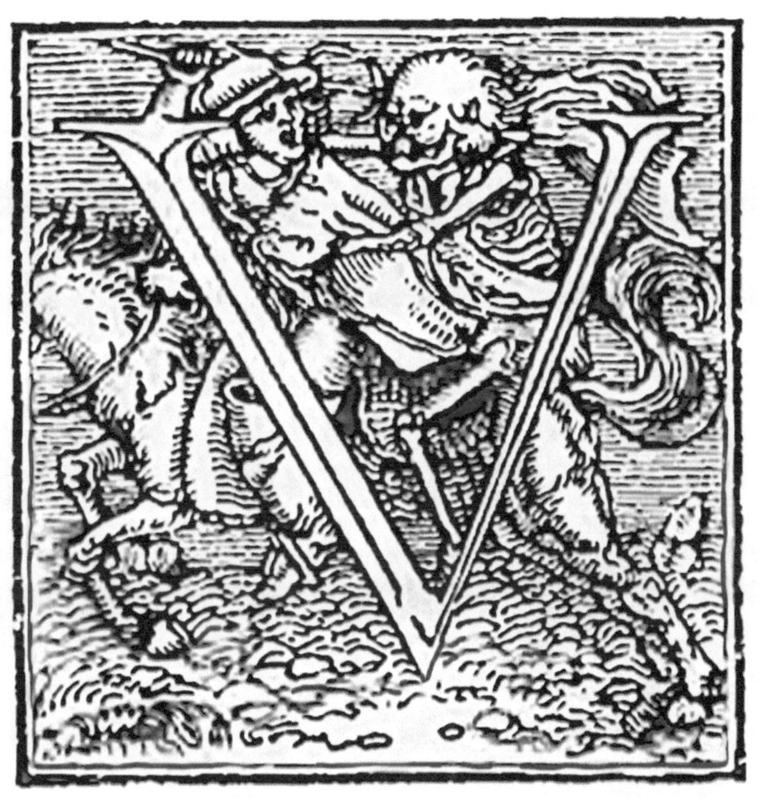

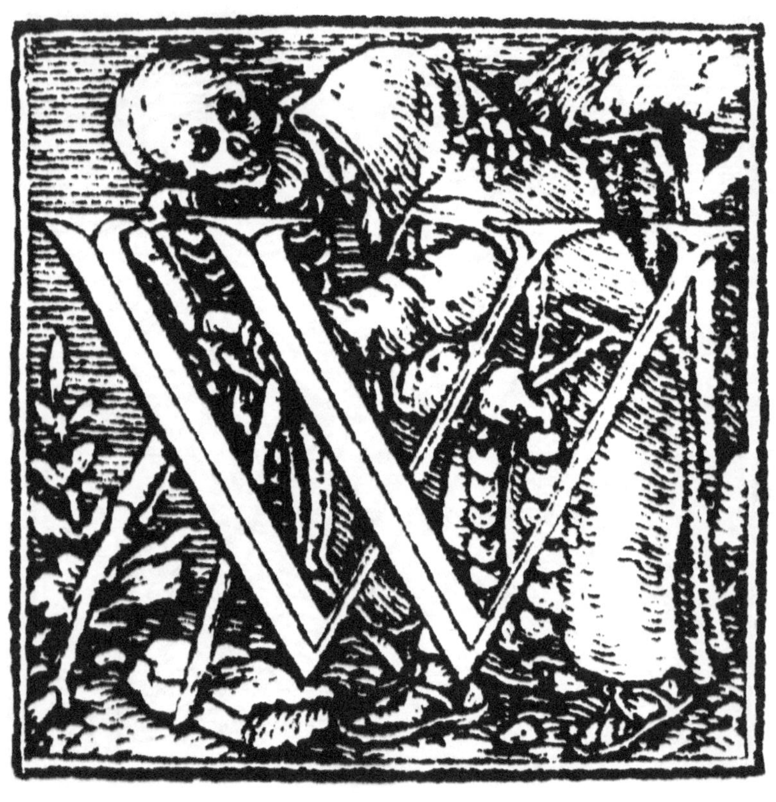

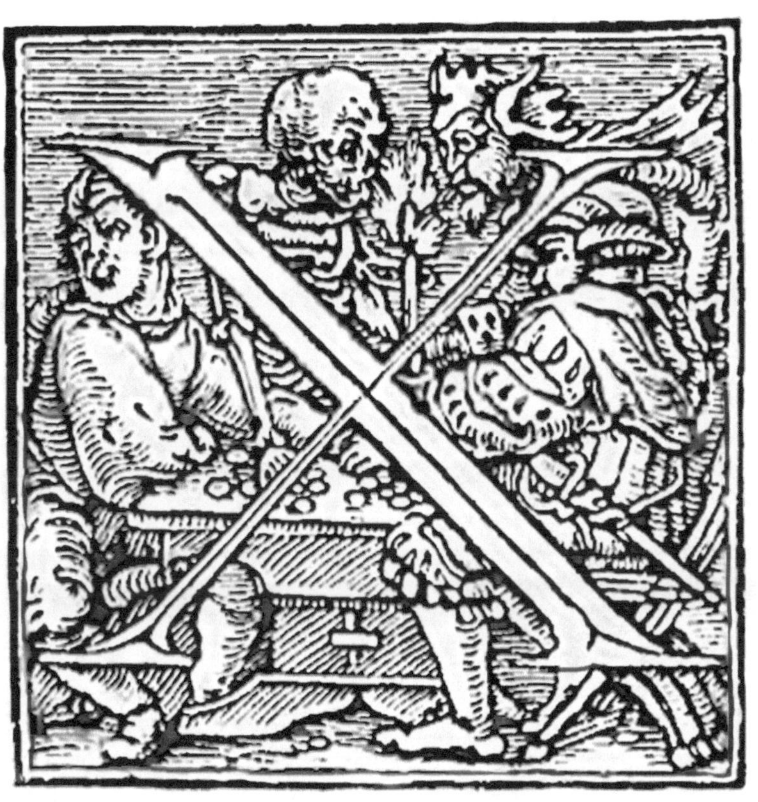

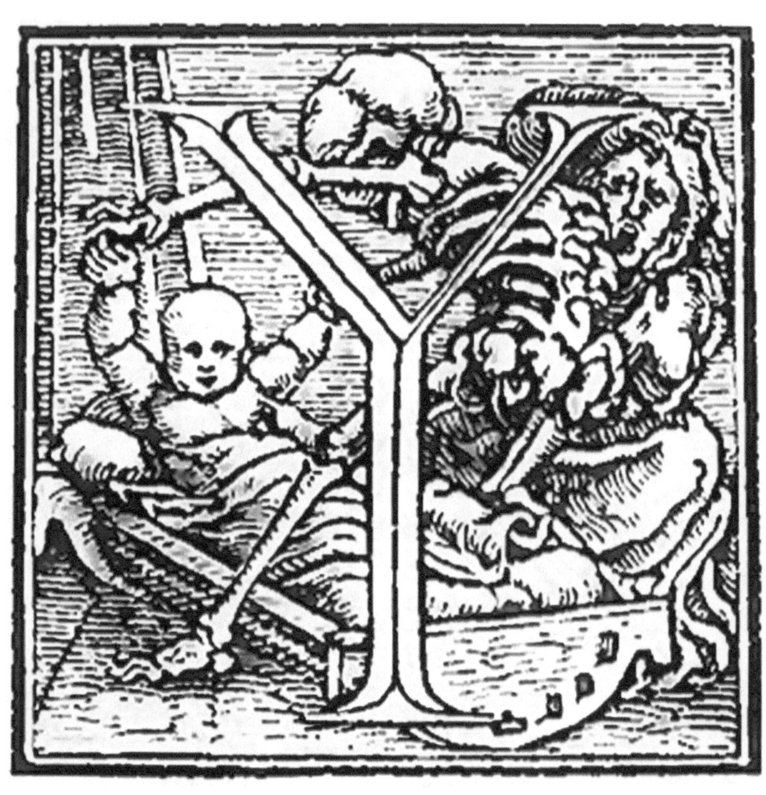

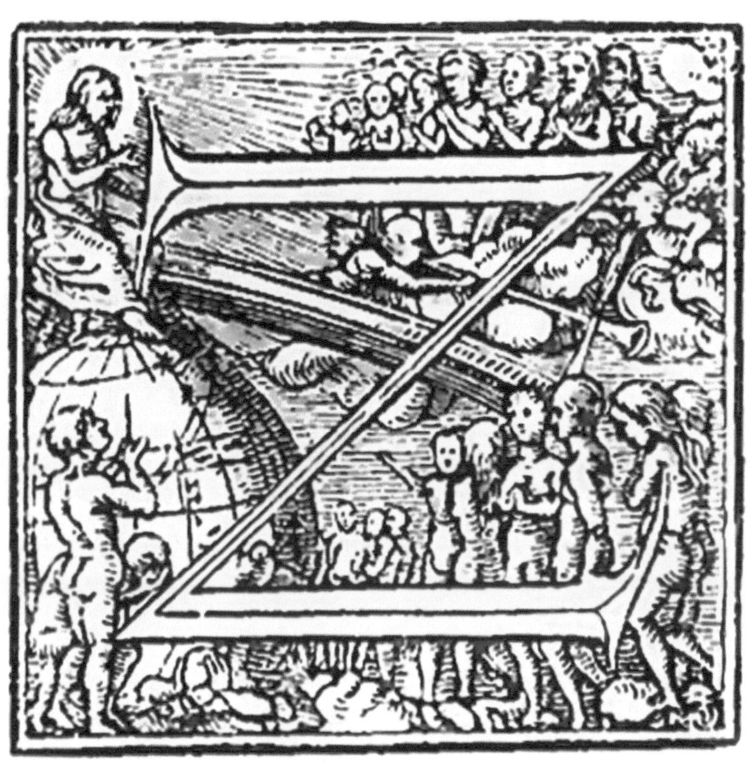